THE PROFESSIONAL ASSISTANT

A GUIDE TO SUCCESS FOR REAL ESTATE ASSISTANTS

by

Monica Reynolds

Linda Rosen

with Evan M. Butterfield, MA, JD

With the Endorsement of the
NATIONAL ORGANIZATION OF REAL ESTATE ASSISTANTS (N.O.R.A.℠)

The **National Organization of Real Estate Assistants** (**NORA**SM) fully endorses *The Professional Assistant*, by Monica Reynolds and Linda Rosen. This book meets the high standards set by NORA for professional training of real estate assistants and for instruction leading to the Accredited Residential Assistant (ARA) designation. Those interested in further information regarding ARA designation and NORA may call (612) 475-0797.

Publisher: Carol Luitjens
Senior Real Estate Writer: Evan M. Butterfield, M.A., J.D.
Cover Design: Salvatore Concialdi

Published by Real Estate Education Company®,
a division of Dearborn Financial Publishing, Inc.®
155 North Wacker Drive
Chicago, Illinois 60606-1719
(312) 836-4400
http://www.real-estate-ed.com

Printed in the United States of America.

10 9 8 7 6

Library of Congress Cataloging-in-Publication Data

Reynolds, Monica.
The professional assistant : a guide to success for real estate assistants / Monica Reynolds & Linda Rosen.
p. cm.
Includes bibliographical references and index.
ISBN 0-7931-1774-7
1. Real estate agents — Training of — United States — Handbooks, manuals, etc. 2. Real estate business — United States — Examinations, questions, etc. I. Rosen, Linda. II. Title. III. Title: Guide to success for real estate assistants
HD278.R523 1996
333.33'076 — dc20 95-50124
CIP

Contents

Preface

As any real estate assistant can tell you, nothing ever gets done without teamwork. The agent may have an office wall covered with awards and certificates recognizing his or her outstanding performance, but the assistant knows (and so does the agent) that none of those professional accomplishments would have been possible — or at least they would have been a lot more difficult to attain — without the assistant's help.

This book is the result of teamwork, too: the authors, publisher and reviewers all worked together to assemble the best possible guide to achieving success as a real estate assistant. From start to finish, this book was written with *you* in mind. Congratulations on picking the right team, and good luck in your professional career!

About the Authors

Monica Reynolds has been a real estate agent since 1980. She hired her first assistant in 1984. At the time, the average sales price in her area was $70,000, and her production went from $3 million to $6 million in one year; it increased to $9 million the next. She was the top agent in North Dakota. In 1989, Walter Sanford convinced her to move to California to put her organizational and checklist systems to work for him. She revamped the organization, managed and trained the assistants and implemented systems to control costs and increase income. Today, she is one of the top motivational speakers in the industry, and appears before two thousand agents a month. She is the author of *The Real Estate Assistant Manual* and *Multiply Your Success with Real Estate Assistants*. She has produced a six-cassette audio package on the subject of real estate assistants. Monica also owns "800 Powerline," a lead generating system with an 800 number. Monica Reynolds can be contacted at P.O. Box 10143, Newport Beach, California 92658 (714) 759-1179.

Linda Rosen founded the National Organization of Real Estate Assistants (NORA℠) to professionalize, educate and designate real estate assistants. NORA's two-day Accredited Residential Assistant (ARA) program is currently being offered throughout the U.S., and will soon be offered in Canada. The program is designed to encourage assistants to act as business managers for real estate agents, to develop a sound structure and expand the business not only in volume but in customer service, professionalism, marketing, computers and systems. Rosen, who created the ARA designation class, conducts the program nationwide. She currently operates the Linda Rosen Institute in Minneapolis, a consulting and training firm that specializes in real estate business management, marketing, team development and assistant issues. She has created a series of agent and team development products under the trademark REALASAURUS™. She is a licensed real estate agent, and worked for over four years as a licensed business manager and marketing director for a $28 million producer.

Editorial Review Board

The following people provided invaluable professional guidance in prepaing this book:

Rebekah and Gene Rivers, GRI, CRS, LTG, ABR, CRP are the only accredited instructors for the Florida Real Estate Commission's CE course, and the Florida Association of REALTORS®' GRI Masters Course on real estate assistants. Actively involved with NAR committees and organizations at the national state and local level, Rebekah and Gene are frequent public speakers and have received numerous awards for performance and expertise, including Tallahassee Board of REALTORS® REALTOR® of the Year. They are Tallahassee Board of REALTORS® and Florida Association of REALTORS® Honor Society Designees. They operate a successful real estate office in Tallahassee which represents sales volume in the top 1 percent of all REALTORS® nationally.

Elaine K. Houser, M.Ed., has served as Education Director of the REALTORS® Association of Metropolitan Pittsburgh and of the REALTORS® Educational Institute since 1988. She holds a Master of Education Degree in Educational Leadership from Carlow College, Pennsylvania School Principal Certification, and is a licensed Pennsylvania real estate salesperson. Elaine has been active in education for over 25 years as a teacher, curriculum writer and school administrator. She is a member of NAR's Education Forum, and has been appointed to the Volunteer Education Advisory Committee for the Pennsylvania Real Estate Commission and the Advisory Team of the Allegheny Policy Council on Education. She also serves as an Education Consultant for the Teacher Assessment Center at Carlow College, Pittsburgh.

Marilyn D. Glazer, GRI, CRS, CRB is an instructor for real estate broker pre-licensing, continuing education and sales training, conducting over 200 courses a year. She has also instituted a Personal Assistant Certificate program from local community colleges. A past president of the North Shore Board of REALTORS® and of Women in Real Estate, Glazer is also an active member of the Illinois Association of REALTORS®, the National Association of REALTORS®, Women's Council of REALTORS® and the Real Estate Educators Association. Her professional honors include REALTOR® Associate and REALTOR® of the Year for the North Shore Board of REALTORS® and REALTOR® of the Year for the Illinois Association of REALTORS®. She is the owner of her own brokerage, Marilyn D. Glazer, REALTOR®, Skokie, and is President of Glazer Enterprises, Inc., and a partner in Trio Productions, Inc.

Barney Fletcher, M.B.A. owns the largest private real estate school in Georgia, and is the author of several Georgia-specific real estate training guides. Barney received his bachelor's degree in business administration from the University of Georgia, and his M.B.A. from Georgia State University, majoring in Real Estate and Urban Affairs. He is a charter member of the Real Estate Education Association

Timothy A. Baker, GRI, CRS, CRP is a co-broker owner of RE/MAX Affiliates, Naperville, Illinois. He has spoken at the National Association of REALTORS® convention and at real estate gatherings across the country. He is featured on the Howard Brinton Star of the Month Club tapes, and has written articles for *Real Estate Today*, *Real Estate Professional* and the*RE/MAX Times*, and has been featured on the RE/MAX Satellite Network. Tim employs two licensed assistants and five unlicensed assistants in his yearly production of over $30 million annually.

Evan M. Butterfield, MA, JD is a professional writer, editor, instructor and a licensed attorney. As Real Estate Education Company's Senior Real Estate Writer, he has worked on state and national editions of *Modern Real Estate Practice* and the publisher's continuing education series.

Introduction

WHAT IS A PROFESSIONAL REAL ESTATE ASSISTANT?[1]

According to a recent survey conducted by the National Association of REALTORS®, most of the largest real estate brokerage firms in the United States currently employ professional real estate assistants. That means that the top money-makers in the real estate industry recognize the importance of assistants to their success: but just what *is* a real estate assistant? First, let's consider what an assistant is *not*. A professional real estate assistant is *not* a secretary, and *not* a telemarketer. An assistant is not someone who takes phone messages or who simply manages the day-to-day operations of a real estate office.

Having said what an assistant is not, however, it should be noted that all of these things figure, to some degree, in the assistant's job description. But there's more. Real estate agents get bogged down with paperwork, multiple listing details, handling non-productive telephone calls, meeting with inspectors and a thousand other details. While these jobs are very important, they prevent the agent from achieving his or her full earning potential. Savvy agents are turning to real estate assistants for help. Today's real estate assistant is a trained (and often licensed) professional, with strong credentials and a diverse background of qualifications. But what do they do?

First and foremost, an assistant's role is to keep his or her agent active on the front line, face to face with buyers and sellers. Here are some of the typical tasks performed by a personal assistant in a top-producing real estate office:

- Make listing appointments
- Prepare documents
- Meet with appraisers
- Receptionist
- Input listings onto a Multiple Listing Service
- Update client records
- Hold open houses
- Attend closings
- Conduct market analyses
- Develop advertising strategies
- Maintain filing systems
- Produce correspondence

---

1 "Real estate assistants" are also referred to as *personal assistants*, *professional assistants* and *PAs*. In this book, we will use the term *real estate assistant* or simply *assistant*.

- Produce flyers and other advertising materials
- Monitor listings
- Direct incoming calls and mail
- Respond to phone and walk-in inquiries
- Maintain business supplies
- Handle checking accounts, deposits, reconciliations
- Communicate with past clients
- Post new listings and sales
- Prospect for buyers and sellers
- Communicate with FSBOs (For-Sale-By-Owner)
- Work with sellers and buyers in all aspects of a transaction, start to finish
- Telemarketing

As you can see, it's a wide-ranging list of responsibilities. Some of these jobs require a real estate license; some demand a basic understanding of computer technology; others require basic accounting or communication skills. Many require creativity and sound business sense. A personal assistant needs to have broad-based training and an arsenal of skills in addition to a positive attitude and a willingness to learn, to achieve, and to work effectively with the real estate team.

HOW TO USE *THE PROFESSIONAL ASSISTANT*

At the beginning of each chapter you'll find a preview of the major topics covered, as well as some **objectives** — specific things you should be able to do once you've mastered the material. At the end of each chapter is a series of **review questions** to test your comprehension. You can check your answers in the **answer key** at the end of this book, and increase your vocabulary with the **glossary**. If you want to learn more about some of the subjects covered, a list of recommended **further readings** is provided. Throughout the book, **examples**, **figures**, **forms** and other **illustrations** are also used to clarify and explain the material. In addition, the following **icons** are used to signal special information:

Some of an assistant's tasks require a real estate license. Where the book addresses such issues, the **license icon** appears. *As the number of states that regulate the activities of real estate assistants increases, these issues are of greater and greater importance!*

The **bright idea icon** *tells you that the accompanying text provides on-the-job advice: a relevant tip or creative shortcut to help you be more successful.*

The quote icon lets you know that you're reading a real-world quote froma practicing personal assistant or real estate agent about the topic being discussed

1

Real Estate Agents and the Real Estate Industry

In this chapter, we will consider the basic structure of the real estate industry: how it's organized and governed, what roles are played by brokers, salespersons, professional associations and state commissions.

We'll also look at the important issue of agency as it applies to real estate licensees — that is, just whom does the broker or salesperson represent, and what are the duties and responsibilities of that representation? By the end of the chapter, you should be able to recognize the basic forms of agency, and explain the concept of fiduciary duty. You should also understand the fair housing laws and standards of ethical practice that affect the real estate industry.

Throughout the chapter, you will be introduced to some of the basic language of real estate. Like any other profession, real estate has its own jargon, its own special-use terms and shorthand ways of expressing complicated ideas. By the end of the chapter, you should be able to understand the fundamental terminology of the real estate industry.

THE REAL ESTATE INDUSTRY

The real estate industry is one of the largest in the United States, employing millions of people in a wide variety of jobs. Of course, there are real estate agents — brokers and salespeople whose job it is to bring buyers and sellers together. But there are many others involved as well: lawyers, appraisers and inspectors, for example. There are also developers, architects and builders; lending institutions and mortgage brokers. Even real estate agents have begun to specialize, creating new niches in the profession: transactional brokers and buyer's brokers, for example. In later chapters, we'll be focusing on the vital role the professional real estate assistant plays in this huge industry; for now, we'll work on understanding the industry as a whole: who are they players, and what are the rules of the game.

Real Estate: A Regulated Profession

At the state government level, the real estate profession is regulated by a **state real estate commission**, whose job it is to write and enforce the rules that govern the way real estate agents do business. The real estate commissions are given authority over the industry by their state's **legislature**, and the legislature also passes laws that govern real estate transactions. Local communities may also enact laws effecting real estate transactions (for example, some local ordinances bar the display of yard signs).

The federal government is also involved: antidiscrimination laws (discussed later in this chapter), along with banking, insurance and environmental regulations have a significant impact on the real estate industry; so does the interest rate set by the Federal Reserve, which determines how affordable mortgage loans will be for borrowers. In addition to regulating the behavior and business practices of real estate professionals, the federal, state and local governments are also taxing bodies. **Taxes** are imposed on the transfer of real estate, and gains and losses from real estate transactions have significant tax aspects as well. Most significant is the home mortgage deduction, which permits homeowners to deduct the interest paid on residential mortgages from their income taxes: this is often viewed as a major factor in the home buying decision.

Self-Regulation: Professional Associations

In addition to government regulation, the real estate industry is also **self-regulating** — that is, it establishes rules and practices for itself. Self-regulation is accomplished through professional organizations such as the **National Association of REALTORS®**, or NAR, the largest of the professional organizations. The 800,000 members of NAR subscribe to a Code of Ethics designed to ensure the fair and honest treatment of both the public and other professionals. Only members of NAR are entitled to be referred to as **REALTORS®** or **REALTOR-ASSOCIATES®**, which are protected trademarks. NAR also has regional, state, county and municipal associations or boards.

Another professional society is the 5,000-member *National Association of Real Estate Brokers* (NAREB). Members of NAREB are known as *Realtists*, and also subscribe to a code of ethics. Other professional associations include the Appraisal Institute, the Building Owners and Managers Association (BOMA), the National Association of Independent Fee Appraisers, the American Institute of Real Estate Appraisers, the American Land Development Association, the Real Estate Educators Association (REEA) and the Real Estate Buyer's Agent Council (REBAC).

Professional Designations

NAR offers a variety of **designations** that its members may use in addition to the REALTORS® designation. For example, an agent's name may be followed by "GRI." GRI stands for "Graduate, REALTORS® Institute," and means that the agent has successfully completed an approved course sponsored by his or her state association. Courses are offered in a variety of areas of professional interest, such as law, appraisal, finance and office management. A Certified Property Manager (CPM) is a professional property manager who has completed the course work and examination requirements of NAR's Institute of Real Estate Management. Commercial real estate practitioners may be members of the Commercial Investment Real Estate Institute (CIREI), and may be designated as a CCIM (Certified Commercial Investment Member). The American Society of Real Estate Counselors offers the CRE (Counselor of Real Estate) designation to members. Agents who specialize in land transactions may be members of the REALTORS® Land Institute (RLI), which offers the Accredited Land Consultant (ALC) designation. The goal of the Real Estate Brokerage Counsel is to improve professionalism in the management of real estate brokerage offices; its members may be awarded a CRBM — Certified Real Estate Brokerage Manager. The REALTORS® National Marketing Institute is an educational organization that offers three designations: CCIM (Certified Commercial and Investment Member), CRB (Certified Residential Broker), and CRS (Certified Residential Salesperson). REEA offers the DREI (Designated Real Estate Instructor) designation to outstanding educators, while a real estate professional who completes an intensive course of study with BOMA may be certified as an RPA, or Real Property Administrator. Members of the Institute of Real Estate Management (IREM) may be designated as Accredited Resident Manager (ARM). There are many more professional societies, educational institutions, and designations. The Real Estate Buyer's Agent Council offers members the Accredited Buyer's Representative (ABR) designation to buyer's agents. (See Chapter 3 for a discussion of the Accredited Residential Assistant (ARA) designation and other training options available to real estate assistants.)

These designations indicate that an individual has devoted his or her time and energy to professional growth and development in one or more areas of interest. Similarly, participation in a local, state or national professional organization indicates an interest in networking, sharing ideas and in strengthening the real estate profession. An observant real estate assistant will be aware of which organizations his or her broker or sales associate belongs to: they are good indicators of the agent's interests.

LICENSING REQUIREMENTS

The requirements for a real estate broker or salesperson's license vary from state to state. In all states, an individual who wants to be a real estate salesperson must take one or more **prelicense classes** (anywhere from 30 to 90 hours or more on the basics of the real estate industry, real estate law and practices, agency and mathematics) and then pass a written examination. Brokers must take additional course work, have practiced as salespersons for some period of time and pass a more detailed exam.

Once a broker or salesperson has passed the licensing exam, however, his or her training has not ended. Most states have a **continuing education** (CE) requirement for real estate licensees. That is, they must take one or more approved classes prior to renewing their license. In this way, state legislatures and commissions hope to ensure that all the state's licensees are aware of current developments in real estate law, and are aware of new trends and practices. The ultimate goal of continuing education is to protect the public from uninformed and unprofessional practitioners.

Real estate assistants should be aware of their state's CE and post-licensing education requirements, as well as particular CE courses that may be of interest to their employers. Of course, a real estate assistant who holds a real estate license must comply with all CE regulations. Local real estate schools or professional organizations can send you information about their CE offerings.

Broker versus Salesperson

A **real estate broker** is a licensed professional who, for a fee or commission, acts as an intermediary on behalf of another person in the sale or purchase of real property. There are several distinct parts to this definition, each of which is important on its own. First, the broker is *licensed.* He or she has satisfied the experience, education and character requirements set by the state, and has been given the right to represent others in a real estate transaction. Of course, anyone can represent anyone else, which brings us to the second part of the definition: *for a fee or commission.* Under most state laws, anyone who is paid to act as an intermediary in a real estate transaction must be licensed. The broker is an *intermediary*: he or she may represent the buyer or the seller, but in either case the broker stands in someone else's shoes — in the sale of a house, for instance, the broker markets the property, the broker shows it to potential buyers, the broker presents the offer and the broker manages the closing. The home owner could do all that alone, of course, and many do. But if a home owner hires a broker, the broker acts on the home owner's behalf throughout the transaction.

A **real estate salesperson**, on the other hand, is a licensed professional who, for some sort of compensation, is employed or associated with a broker to perform certain activities with regard to a real estate transaction. The salesperson acts at all times on behalf of the broker who is his or her employer. While the salesperson may make the listing presentation in the seller's home, it is the broker who takes the ultimate responsibility for the salesperson's actions. The broker shares commissions with the salespeople.

In some real estate offices, the salespeople are **employees**: they are paid a regular salary and receive benefits; they use the broker's facilities and equipment. In other offices, the salespeople are **independent contractors**: they pay for all their expenses and employment taxes, and receive no benefits from the broker. On the other hand, they are not subject to the broker's control with regard to how they market properties, and typically retain a larger share of the commission they earn.

Commissions

Real estate brokers make their living through commissions. A **commission** is usually a percentage of the selling price of a property, or it may be a flat fee, paid to the broker for services rendered in the sale or purchase of the property. The amount of the commission is agreed upon by the seller (or buyer) and the broker in advance, usually in writing in the listing agreement. It must be freely negotiated, and may not be "set" by any association. If multiple brokers are involved in a transaction — that is, there is a listing broker who obtained the right to market the property and a selling broker who actually found the buyers — the commission will usually be split in some way. Usually, the amount of shared commission is stated in the listing, so cooperating brokers know in advance what their interest will be.

A commission is generally considered to be "earned" when the work for which the broker was hired is accomplished: that is, when a completed and binding sales contract has been entered into by the buyer and seller. The broker must produce a "ready, willing and able buyer" — a person who wishes to buy on the seller's terms, and who takes positive steps toward closing the transaction. Even if the sale does not close, the broker may be entitled to a commission if the deal fell apart due to some action by the principal.

A salesperson is compensated by some arrangement with his or her employing broker. The broker may pay the salesperson a salary plus a percentage of commissions earned, while some firms have adopted a 100-percent commission plan, under which salespersons pay the broker a monthly charge to cover the cost of their desk and office services in return for keeping the entire commission paid from sales they negotiate. In either case, the compensation may be paid *only by the employing broker.*

In most states, unlicensed real estate assistants are not permitted to receive any part of a commission. This is usually a matter of brokerage policy in compliance with state regulations, which vary from state to state. Some licensed assistants are compensated only in the form of a commission, while others receive a base salary for their non-licensed activities plus a commission for their "real estate" work. In some offices, assistants are paid on an hourly basis only. Some assistants may receive a salary plus a transaction bonus.

LISTINGS

The employment contract between a broker and a seller is called a **listing agreement**. It is an agreement that the broker will provide his or her professional services in return for the payment of a commission. *A listing agreement is a "personal services contract" — it is* not *a real estate contract.* A salesperson may present a listing agreement for a seller's signature, but only in the name of his or her broker. Under the laws of most states, the listing agreement must be in writing to be enforceable in court, although oral agreements are often permissible. Listing agreements may also be referred to as *marketing* or *employment agreements.*

There are several different types of listing agreements. The type of contract determines the specific rights and obligations of each party.

In an **exclusive right to sell** listing, one broker is appointed as the sole representative of the seller to market the seller's property for a certain period of time. If the property is sold while the contract is in effect, the seller must pay the broker a commission *regardless of who sells the property.*

...FOR EXAMPLE

Broker A entered into a 90-day listing agreement with Owner. If Broker A produces a buyer within 90 days, she is owed a commission. If Broker C produces a buyer, Broker A gets the commission (and shares it with Broker C). Even if Owner decides to sell his house to his neighbor's daughter two weeks after the listing is signed, Broker A is still owed a commission. Finally, if Broker A shows the property to Buyer during the listing period, and Buyer negotiates a purchase after the listing agreement expires, Broker A may nonetheless be owed a commission.

In an **exclusive agency listing**, the seller authorizes one broker as his or her representative, but retains the right to sell the property by him or herself without obligation to the broker. On the other hand, in an **open listing** agreement (also known as a *nonexclusive* or *general listing*), the seller retains the right to employ several brokers simultaneously, and to market the property by him or herself. The seller is obligated to pay a commission only to the broker who is the first to successfully produce a ready, willing and able buyer. Of course, if the seller sells the property without the assistance of a broker, he or she is not obliged to pay anyone.

A **net listing** specifies an amount of money that the seller will receive from the sale of his or her property. The broker is free to offer the property at any price higher than the net amount. The broker is entitled to keep any money above the seller's specified net. Because of the possibility of fraud and conflicts of interest, however, net listings are discouraged in most states and illegal in many. Similarly, an **option listing** gives the broker the right to purchase the property, but is also a hotbed of potential conflicts of interest. As we'll discuss later in this chapter, a broker owes certain duties to his client that net and option listings may violate.

MULTIPLE-LISTING SERVICES

A **multiple-listing service** (MLS) is a marketing organization whose broker/members pay a fee to make their own exclusive listings available to other brokers, and gain access to other brokers' listings as well. Multiple listing services are available on computer networks as well as in the form of large printed "catalogs" of available properties.

A multiple listing service offers advantages to both the buyer and the seller. Brokers have access to a large inventory of properties to be sold, and are assured of a commission if they list a property or participate in the sale of another broker's listing. Sellers gain because their property is exposed to a considerably larger market.

The contractual obligations among member brokers vary widely among the many multiple listing organizations. Most provide that the commission is divided between the listing broker and the selling broker, with terms for the division agreed upon individually by the brokers themselves. Under most MLS contracts, the broker is obligated to turn new listings over to the service within a specific period of time, usually less than 72 hours. That means that a broker has 72 hours (or less) in which to market a property exclusively, through his or her own office, without notifying other brokers of its availability. The advantage of a sale during this period is that the listing broker will not need to split the commission with another broker. As a result, the first few days (or even hours) of a listing are often very active ones in the broker's office.

AGENCY LAW

The law of agency defines the rights and duties of the principal and the agent. First, let's consider those two terms. A **principal** is the person who hires and/or delegates a responsibility to another person. That second person is the principal's **agent**. The agent owes the principal certain duties, called **fiduciary duties**. They are:

- *Care*: the agent must exercise a reasonable degree of care while transacting the business entrusted to him or her by the principal.

- *Obedience*: the agent must act in good faith at all times, obeying the principal's instructions as long as they are ethical and legal.

- *Accounting*: the agent must be able to report the status of all funds received from or for the principal.

- *Loyalty*: the agent must place the principal's interests above everyone else's, including the agent's own personal interest.

- *Disclosure*: the agent must keep the principal informed of all relevant facts or information, regardless of whether they are favorable or unfavorable to the principal's position.

An agency relationship may be either **express** (that is, there is a clear written or oral agreement establishing the agency) or **implied** (that is, the principal and agent behave as if there is an agency relationship). An agency may be either general or special. A **general agent** represents the principal in a broad range of matters, and has great freedom of action. A **special agent** is authorized to represent the principal only in one specific act or transaction, under detailed instructions. A salesperson is a special agent; a property manager is a general agent. *Subagency* is an arrangement in which a third party is designated as the agent of an agent, and may also act on behalf of the principal.

It is very important to note that *the source of compensation does not determine agency*. An agency can exist in the absence of a fee (called a **gratuitous agency**).

...FOR EXAMPLE

> You're very busy with an important project. At lunchtime, you give your coworker $5 and ask her to go buy your lunch at a mall's food court. You tell her you want either Chinese food or pizza and something to drink. Your friend calls you from the mall to tell you that only hamburgers or salads are available, and either will cost $6.
>
> Your colleague is your *agent*. You have entrusted her with your decision about what kind of food to eat and what kind of beverage to buy. You have also given her a financial responsibility: the responsibility to spend up to five dollars, and to return the change to you along with the food. Is she a *special agent* or a *general agent*? Is the agreement *express* or *implied*? How has your colleague fulfilled her *fiduciary responsibilities*? How?

Principal's Duties

The agent is not the only party with specific responsibilities. The principal also owes certain duties and responsibilities to the agent. One of these is the duty of **compensation**. In a listing agreement between a seller and a broker, for instance, the seller/principal is obligated to pay the broker a fee when the broker produces a ready, willing and able buyer. The principal also has the duty not to hinder the agent's ability to fulfill the fiduciary responsibilities. This duty of **cooperation** means that the principal must deal with the agent in good faith. The principal may not, for example, withhold information that should be disclosed, or refuse a reasonable offer based on the purchaser's race or religion, as discussed below.

REAL ESTATE AGENCY

In the real estate industry, the concept of agency is extremely important. Many states across the country are revising their agency laws to protect consumers and to clarify the responsibilities of brokers and salespersons. In the past, the broker or salesperson always represented the seller. They buyer was on his or her own, and the theory of **caveat emptor**, or "let the buyer beware," was the rule of business. That has changed in recent years, and real estate professionals must be aware of the changing demands of agency.

Agency laws will vary from state to state, as will the definitions and legal duties of agents, clients and customers in a real estate transaction. Assistants must be aware of the agency laws of their particular state.

Clients and Customers

A real estate agent's principal, whether the buyer or the seller, is referred to as the agent's **client**. A client is owed the fiduciary duties of agency. On the other hand, the agent also owes certain limited duties to third parties, who are his or her **customers**. An agent representing a seller would have the seller as a client. People looking for properties to buy are customers.

An agent's duties to customers include:

- ❖ Reasonable care and skill in performance
- ❖ Honesty and fair dealing
- ❖ Disclosure of all facts that the licensee knows (or could reasonably be expected to know) that materially affect the value or desirability of the property

In some states, the law requires additional disclosures of environmental or health hazards that may be present on the property, such as radon, underground storage tanks, lead paint or asbestos.

Some exaggeration, called **puffing**, is permissible. "Puffing" is the practice of enthusiastically describing the merits of a property, such as its location, beautifully landscaped yard or breath-takingly lovely interior spaces. **Fraud** is the intentional misrepresentation of a material fact in a way that harms or takes advantage of another person. It includes making false statements about a property as well as concealing or failing to disclose important facts. A contract obtained as a result of fraud may be renounced by the purchaser. The broker will lose a commission and be liable for damages if the buyer or seller suffered a loss due to the broker's action.

...FOR EXAMPLE

Broker A showed a house to a prospective purchaser. Broker A pointed out the "gorgeous landscaping," the "charm and elegance" of the dining room and the "perfect" location. This is all permissible puffing.

Broker B showed a different house to a prospective purchaser, but was careful not to mention that the basement always flooded after moderate rainfall. Instead, he agreed with the buyer that the basement would make a wonderful carpeted rec room. This is an example of fraud.

A growing number of state laws require sellers to discover and disclose certain latent defects that threaten the property's structural soundness or the personal safety of its inhabitants. A

latent defect is a hidden defect that would not be discovered by ordinary inspection, and that materially affects the value of the property. Latent defects include such physical elements as cracked foundations, leaking roofs and malfunctioning heating or cooling systems as well as violations of building codes or zoning ordinances. **Stigmatized properties**, such as homes in which a violent or scandalous event has occurred, may or may not be subject to disclosure requirements, depending on state law.

Brokers, salespeople and staff members — including real estate assistants — must be careful about the statements they make to customers. They must be sure that the customer clearly understands whether a statement is a fact or opinion. While state laws vary, the most an unlicensed real estate assistant may do is provide customers with factual information from a listing sheet. Individual offices will have specific policies regarding the sort of information real estate assistants may offer.

Errors and Omissions Insurance. Because of their enormous exposure to liability, some brokers purchase what are known as **errors and omissions insurance policies** for their firms. Some state licensing laws require brokers to obtain such policies. Similar to the malpractice insurance pur-chased by doctors and lawyers, "E&O" policies cover liability for errors, mistakes and negligence in the usual listing and selling of real estate. No insurance protects a real estate professional from litigation arising from criminal acts or violation of civil rights laws.

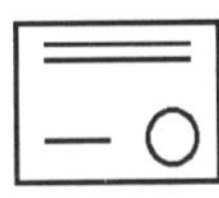

Licensed real estate assistants are typically covered by a broker's E&O insurance policy. Unlicensed real estate assistants, however, are not usually covered. This creates a potential liability exposure for the broker. Insurance companies may negotiate a rider that ensures errors and omissions coverage for unlicensed assistants.

Seller as Principal

If a seller contracts with a broker to market the seller's real estate, the broker becomes the seller's agent. The seller is the principal and the broker's client. A buyer who contacts the broker to view properties is the broker's customer. The listing agreement is the agency contract between the broker and the seller: it usually authorizes the broker to use licensees employed by the broker, as well as other, cooperating brokers in marketing the property.

Buyer as Principal

The practice of buyers hiring brokers to represent their interests in finding real estate is becoming more common. Many brokers are specializing in this field, and are referred to as **buyer's brokers**. This is still an agency relationship, but the buyer is the principal and client, while the seller is the broker's customer. A buyer's broker will generally enter into an **exclusive buyer agency agreement** with the buyer, which is an employment contract establishing the terms and conditions of the agency relationship. The buyer may pay a fee for the buyer broker's services, and the buyer broker may received a percentage of the commission as a cooperating broker.

Under many states' laws, an agency relationship may be established even in the absence of a buyer agency agreement, based only on the perceptions and actions of the parties. In a growing number of states, a broker is legally the agent of the party with whom he or she is working, whether buyer or seller.

Owner as Principal

An owner may employ a broker to market, lease, maintain or manage the owner's property. This is known as **property management**. The broker is the owner's agent for purposes of marketing the property to potential tenants, collecting rents, supervising maintenance or managing the day-to-day operations of the owner's commercial or residential property, depending on the scope and terms of the property management agreement.

Single Agency

In a single-agency relationship, the broker represents either the buyer or the seller in a transaction. Any other party is a customer. A single-agency broker may represent both buyers and sellers, or may specialize in one or the other. However, in any individual transaction, the broker represents only one party.

Dual Agency

In some states, it is permissible for a single broker to represent both the buyer and the seller in a real estate transaction. In these cases, called **disclosed dual agency**, the buyer and seller must be informed that the broker will represent both parties, and must consent to the arrangement. The buyer and seller must be more cautious in protecting their interests, and the broker must figure out a way to provide both parties with the fiduciary duties of an agent. Protecting confidential information is a particular challenge: the top price the buyer may ultimately be willing to pay, for example, would be of great interest to the seller, as would the seller's bottom line be highly relevant to the buyer.

A broker may not create a dual agency without first disclosing it to the parties. An **undisclosed dual agency** violates state licensing laws, and can result in a sales contract falling through, commissions being forfeited, and even lawsuits. While the dual agency may be unintentional or accidental — the result of carelessness or over-enthusiasm — it is not permissible.

Transactional Brokers

Some brokers avoid the possibility of undisclosed dual agency by acting as **transactional or facilitating brokers**: they provide buyers and sellers with the paperwork and objective professional guidance necessary to transfer ownership of real property without establishing an agency relationship. The buyer and seller may negotiate directly with each other, or through the broker, but the broker does not represent either of the parties.

FAIR HOUSING

Real estate licensees are subject to a number of local, state and federal civil rights and antidiscrimination laws, referred to as **fair housing laws**. At the federal level, these include the Civil Rights Act of 1866, which prohibits any type of discrimination based on race. The **Fair Housing Act** (which includes Title VIII of the Civil Rights Act of 1968, the 1974 Housing and Community Development Act, and the Fair Housing Amendments Act of 1988) prohibits housing discrimination based on the following factors:

- race
- color
- religion
- sex
- handicap (including AIDS)
- familial status (that is, marital status or family size)
- national origin

Some state laws also provide protections based on economic factors, such as receiving housing subsidies or public aid payments. Sexual preference is protected in some states.

In short, it is illegal to discriminate against persons in the protected classes by changing the way properties are offered for sale or rent; by refusing to rent or sell; or by changing terms or conditions of sale, rental or lending. If any aspect of a real estate transaction is different because of the status of the purchaser as a member of a protected class, the act is likely to be illegal.

Blockbusting

It is unlawful for a real estate professional to encourage, or attempt to encourage, anyone to sell or rent their property because a member of the protected classes is moving into the neighborhood. Any action that conveys the spoken or unspoken message that the neighborhood is "changing" is considered **blockbusting**, and is illegal.

Steering

Potential home buyers may not be channeled or directed toward particular neighborhoods. **Steering** includes showing homes to members of certain ethnic groups only in areas in which there are significant numbers of that group already living as well as steering to change the character of a neighborhood. The salesperson's role is to determine home seekers' financial capabilities and personal housing desires and requirements, and to show them homes objectively, based on those factors alone.

Advertising

Printed or published advertising of property for sale or rent may not include language that indicates a preference or limitation, regardless of how subtle the choice of words. Pictures of models as residents or customers must be reasonably inclusive, and may not depict one segment of the population exclusively. The media used for promoting property or real estate services may not target one population to the exclusion of others.

PROFESSIONAL ETHICS

Professional conduct involves more than just complying with the federal, state and local laws regulating the real estate industry. The term "**ethics**" refers to a system of moral principles, rules and standards of conduct. The ethical system adopted by a profession — the physicians' Hippocratic Oath; the lawyers' Canons of Ethics — establishes conduct that exceeds simply complying with the laws. In the real estate industry, members of the nation's largest trade association, the National Association of REALTORS®, subscribe to a strict code of conduct called the Code of Ethics and Standards of Practice. Other industry organizations have codes of ethics as well.

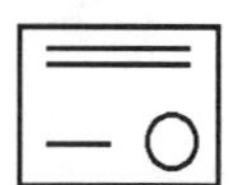

Real estate assistants who hold real estate licenses may be members of the NAR, in which case they will be governed by the NAR's Code of Ethics. The Code is revised from time to time: a copy of the current Code of Ethics may be obtained from the National Association of REALTORS®, 430 North Michigan Avenue, Chicago, Illinois 60611. An unlicensed real estate assistant whose employer is a REALTOR® should conduct him or herself in accordance with the ethical standards expected of his or her employer.

PUTTING IT ALL TOGETHER

Regulation, licensing, agency and ethics — when you add them up, they form the framework for a days' work in the real estate industry. How brokers and salespeople interact with each other and with the public is dictated by law and ethical considerations.

How they interact with their clients and customers depends on the law of agency. The diagram below illustrates the process of how a home is sold. You should study it carefully, for everything you do as a professional real estate assistant in a real estate office will take place somewhere on that flowchart. By now, you should have a fairly clear idea of the theories behind real estate practice. From here on, we'll be closely considering the real estate assistant's role in the real estate industry.

Figure 1.1 The Anatomy of a Real Estate Transaction

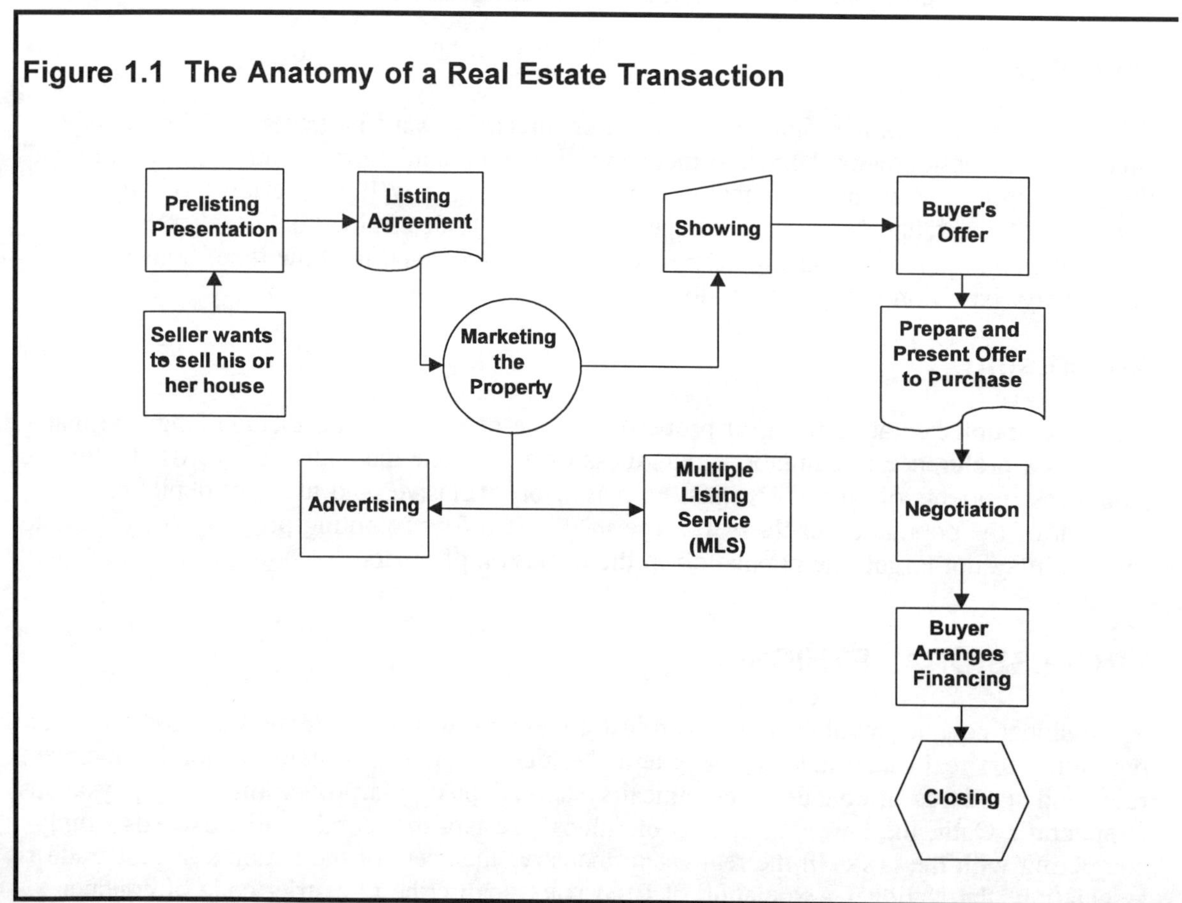

SUMMARY

The real estate industry is one of the largest in the United States. The profession is regulated at the state level by a real estate commission, and is also subject to other state, local and federal laws. In addition, professional organizations provide self-regulation and a variety of professional designations that demonstrate expertise and special training.

Real estate brokers and salespeople must be licensed by their state. The licensing process involves a demonstration of good character, satisfaction of an education requirement and passing a licensing examination. Periodic continuing education may also be necessary. The licensing requirements for brokers and salespeople are different, and they have different roles in the real estate office.

The law of agency defines the rights and duties of a principal and agent. An agent owes his or her principal the fiduciary duties of care, obedience, accounting, loyalty and disclosure. The principal owes the agent compensation and cooperation. An agency may be express or implied, and does not depend on who pays the agent. The principal is the agent's client, but the agent owes customers the duties of reasonable care and skill, honesty and fair dealing, and disclosure of material facts. An agency may be single or dual; either the seller or the buyer may be the principal.

Real estate licensees are subjects to a variety of local, state and federal civil rights and antidiscrimination laws known as fair housing laws. The laws bar discrimination in housing transactions against certain protected classes of individuals. In addition, real estate professionals may be required by their professional society to adhere to certain ethical practices.

KEY TERMS

agent
blockbusting
buyer's broker
client
commission
compensation
continuing education
cooperating broker
customers
designations
dual agency
employees
errors and omissions
ethics
exclusive agency
exclusive right to sell
express agency
Fair Housing Act
fair housing laws
fiduciary duties
fraud
general agent
gratuitous agency
implied agency
independent contractors
latent defect
legislature
listing agreement
listing broker
multiple listing service
National Association of REALTORS®
net listing
open listing
option listing
prelicensing classes
principal
property management
puffing
real estate salesperson
real estate broker
self-regulating
state real estate commission
stigmatized properties
Realtists
REALTORS®
special agent
steering
taxes
transactional brokers

Review Questions

1. At the state level, the real estate industry is regulated by the
   a. National Association of REALTORS®.
   b. state real estate commission.
   c. Real Estate Brokerage Council.
   d. state code of ethics.

2. All licensed real estate professionals are
   a. called Realtists.
   b. referred to as real estate brokers.
   c. either REALTORS® or REALTOR-ASSOCIATES®.
   d. either brokers or salespersons.

3. The compensation paid to a broker that is a percentage of the selling price of a property is referred to as a
   a. salary.
   b. listing fee.
   c. commission.
   d. bonus.

4. People who pay all their own expenses and taxes, receive no benefits and are only minimally supervised are known as
   a. real estate employees.
   b. independent contractors.
   c. real estate assistants.
   d. real estate salespersons.

5. *R* asks *Q* to sell *R*'s house. *R* will pay *Q* a commission in return for *Q* using her professional skills and expertise to market the property. *V* comes into *Q*'s office and wants to buy *R*'s house. Which of the following statements is *true*?
   a. *R* is the principal, *Q* is the agent and *V* is the client.
   b. *R* is the client, *Q* is the agent and *V* is the principal.
   c. *R* is the principal, *Q* is the agent and *V* is the customer.
   d. *R* is the client, *Q* is the principal and *V* is the fiduciary.

6. As a rule, unlicensed real estate assistants are permitted to
   a. provide customers with factual information from a listing sheet.
   b. engage in legitimate "puffing" with regard to a specific property.
   c. conceal unpleasant facts about a property's condition.
   d. provide no information to anyone.

7. The federal Fair Housing Act does *not* prohibit discrimination on the basis of
   a. marital status.
   b. sex.
   c. religion.
   d. public aid.

8. Encouraging Asian buyers to locate in particular parts of town with high Asian populations is an example of
   a. steering.
   b. blockbusting.
   c. fair housing.
   d. ethical behavior.

9. A real estate assistant who does not hold a real estate license
   a. may engage in unethical conduct, because he or she is not bound by any standards.
   b. should follow the ethical standards expected of his or her employer.
   c. is not expected to behave ethically.
   d. is never covered by errors and omissions insurance.

10. The ethical system that applies to members of the National Association of REALTORS® is called the
    a. Code of Ethics.
    b. Code of Professional Conduct.
    c. Canons of Real Estate Ethics.
    d. Standards of Ethical Practice.

2

Professional Assistants and the Real Estate Industry

In this chapter, we will examine the important role played by the real estate assistant within the real estate industry generally, and in the day-to-day operation of a real estate office.

We will pay particular attention to the differing responsibilities of licensed and unlicensed real estate assistants, full-time and part-time status and forms of compensation. By the end of the chapter, you should have a clear idea of what a real estate assistant's job is, and what a real estate assistant career would look like. You will know the kinds of expectations you should have and the kinds of questions to ask a potential employer.

WHO IS A REAL ESTATE ASSISTANT?

Real estate assistants first appeared in the real estate industry in the late 1980s. As the real estate industry has changed over the years, so has the job of the real estate assistant. The real estate assistant is changing from a "glorified secretary" to a creative office manager, licensed assistant and licensed business manager.

Ten years ago, finding a part-time job as a real estate assistant for a broker or sales associate was a difficult challenge. Today, as agents find that they cannot deal with the conducting their business *and* engage in self-marketing at the same time, the need for real estate assistants is growing rapidly. The number of available real estate assistants cannot keep pace with the real estate industry's demand for qualified assistants.

NAR Survey

A National Association of REALTORS® survey of the nation's top real estate brokerage firms found widespread employment of real estate assistants. Overall, ten percent of all sales associates have assistants. Large firms (with more than 50 agents) generally employed more than seven assistants, while smaller firms employed one or two. Seventy-four percent of the REALTORS® surveyed by NAR reported that their firms' profitability had increased since employing real estate assistants.

Among the agents, those who employed assistants reported making twice as many listing presentations as those who did not. The agents with assistants obtained a 50 percent greater listing volume and sold more than 60 percent more of their own listings than the other agents.

LICENSING ISSUES

In the National Association of REALTORS® survey discussed earlier, more than half of those with a policy on licensing require their assistants either have a real estate license or strictly avoid any activity for which a license is required. Perhaps reflecting that policy, more than half of the real estate assistants in the industry today have a real estate sales license.

What's the difference between real estate assistants who are licensed and those who are not? As we saw in Chapter 1, the real estate industry in every state is regulated by the state legislature and real estate commission. The real estate laws and regulations in each state clearly define the activities that require a real estate license — usually including virtually all aspects of a real estate agent's activities. Engaging in professional real estate activities without a license is generally illegal, and a broker whose employee violates state real estate law is subject to a range of penalties from a fine to the loss of his or her license. In addition, a real estate assistant who engages in activities for which a real estate license is required is guilty of acting as a broker or salesperson without a license, and may be fined or jailed, depending on the severity of state law and the seriousness of the activity.

As a result, real estate brokerage firms are very cautious when it comes to the responsibilities allowed an assistant.

Unlicensed Real Estate Assistants

The activities an unlicensed real estate assistant may perform are governed by the real estate laws and regulations of each state, as well as determined by office policy. As a general rule, however, an unlicensed assistant may not:

- show properties to prospective buyers
- answer questions about listings, closings, financing or title issues;
- host open houses;
- negotiate on any transaction; or
- receive a commission or percentage of a commission based on a real estate transaction.

An unlicensed assistant may not negotiate, write or amend contracts. He or she may never speak of price, terms or condition of a property to a client or prospective client, and may not solicit for listing presentations on behalf of the agent or discuss financing issues with any client. In short, an unlicensed assistant is not available to "hold down the fort" during the agent's absence.

Of course, an unlicensed assistant can be a useful asset to an agent; both parties simply need to be aware of the legal and policy limitations on his or her activities. Unlicensed assistants are often limited to secretarial services for the sales associate, such as:

- answering phone calls,
- typing letters,
- scheduling appointments,
- assembling closing documents,
- placing signs on properties,
- having duplicate keys made or
- installing lock boxes.

Some real estate firms refuse to hire licensed assistants on the grounds that they don't want to train the competition. For these firms, an unlicensed assistant is more likely to be a "team player" and not someone likely to learn the ropes and then set off on his or her own, taking valuable client contacts along. There are financial considerations as well: it's less expensive to hire an unlicensed assistant than it is to compensate someone who holds a real estate license: the costs of continuing education and licensing fees can add up quickly, particularly for someone who is not, strictly speaking, directly generating commissions.

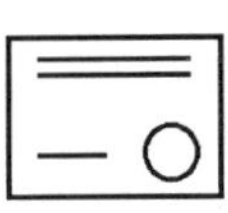

The NAR survey found that the real estate industry as a whole preferred licensed real estate assistants. Nonetheless, there are many unlicensed assistants in the industry, playing an important role in their broker's offices. However, as the industry becomes more accustomed to relying on assistants for a broader range of responsibilities, it is increasingly likely that real estate licenses will become a basic requirement of the job. In addition, a real estate license helps minimize brokers' concerns about possible violations of state regulations by an unlicensed assistant.

Licensed Real Estate Assistants

Many real estate assistants hold real estate licenses, but have chosen not to practice in the field. For some, it's a matter of wanting on-the-job training before they enter a highly competitive profession. Others are more interested in applying their "support" skills in marketing and office management, but feel that a license ensures greater responsibility and more interesting work.

I got my real estate license a year ago. I'd decided about half-way through the exam prep course that I wanted to learn more about the business before I started trying to sell people's houses, even as a salesperson with a broker's supervision. Besides, depending on commissions for my income right now is pretty scary. Being a real estate assistant in a top-selling office is giving me the experience I'll need later on in my career.

For the real estate firm, a licensed assistant is less of a liability: as licensees, they are usually covered by the firm's errors and omissions insurance, and their activities need to be less closely monitored for compliance with the real estate laws. They are also often seen as more valuable, because they can step in for the agent in an emergency or take over more of the time-consuming aspects of the agent's business that nonetheless require a licensee.

EMPLOYMENT ISSUES

A real estate assistant's hours and status in a real estate office are a matter of both office policy and negotiation between the applicant and employer. In general, an individual seeking work as a real estate assistant can choose from a number of work arrangements that offer varying degrees of flexibility, responsibility, independence and compensation.

Employee or Independent Contractor?

The distinction between employees and independent contractors in the context of sales associates was discussed in Chapter 1. The same rules apply to real estate assistants, most of whom are employees.

An **employee** works regular hours as set by the employer; receives a regular salary or per-hour wage; and is entitled to benefits such as insurance, a retirement plan, vacation time and sick leave. An employer is responsible for withholding state and federal income tax, social security (FICA) and other taxes from the employee's paycheck. An employee is entitled to unemployment compensation and worker's compensation for on-the-job injuries. An employee works under the direct supervision of the employer, and is (at least in theory) responsible for carrying out his or her duties in a manner dictated by the employer.

On the other hand, an **independent contractor** is responsible for paying his or her own taxes. He or she works with a minimum of supervision and (within reason) sets his or her own schedule. While the ultimate goal of any task is set by the employer, the methods and procedures used to achieve that goal are up to the independent contractor. The relationship is based on a personal services contract, and the independent contractor is bound by its terms: he or she cannot quit until the job is done, and cannot be fired as long as he or she is in compliance with the contract's terms. The fundamental difference between an employee and an independent contractor is the question of control: who is in charge of the individual's day-to-day activities.

As a rule, any claim that a worker is an independent contractor is likely to subject the relationship to close Internal Revenue Service scrutiny: an unscrupulous employer might use the "independent contractor" label to avoid payroll taxes. The IRS has established guidelines for determining whether or not a worker qualifies as an independent contractor or employee (see Figure 2.1).

I'm a firm believer in hiring assistants as employees. It's just not worth it legally to do it any other way. Plus, the paperwork that is necessary when hiring an independent contractor can be an incredible endeavor.

Figure 2.1 Employee v. Independent Contractor

FACTORS INDICATING CONTROL *Note: These factors are only possible indicators of a worker's status. Each case must be determined on its own facts, based on all the information.*	**EMPLOYEE**	**INDEPENDENT CONTRACTOR**
Is the worker required to comply with **employer instructions** about when, where and how work is to be performed?	Yes	No
Is the worker required to undergo **training**?	Yes	No
Does the worker hire, supervise and pay **others** to perform work for which he or she is responsible?	No	Yes
Must the worker's job be performed during **certain set hours**?	Yes	No
Must the worker devote **full time** to the job?	Yes	No
Must the work be performed **on the employer's property**?	Yes	No
Must tasks be performed in a **certain order** set by the employer?	Yes	No
Is the individual required to submit **regular written or oral reports** to the employer?	Yes	No
Is **payment** by the **hour, week or month**?	Yes	No
Is **payment** in a **lump sum**?	No	Yes
Are the worker's **business and travel expenses** paid by the employer?	Yes	No
Does the employer furnish the **tools and materials** required for the job?	Yes	No
Does the worker rent his or her own **office or working space**?	No	Yes
Will the worker realize a **profit or loss** as a result of his or her services?	No	Yes
Does the individual work for **more than one firm** at a time?	No	Yes
Does the worker make his or her services **available to the general public**?	No	Yes
Does the employer have the **right to fire** the worker?	Yes	No
Does the worker have the **right to quit** the job at any time, whether or not a particular task is complete?	Yes	No

Full-time or Part-time?

The number of hours worked by a real estate assistant is generally a matter of office policy, although individual arrangements may be worked out between the assistant and his or her employing agent. Full-time employees are generally entitled to benefits (such as insurance, vacations and retirement plans), while part-time employees are not. On the other hand, a part-time employee enjoys more time away from the office to spend with his or her family or in other pursuits.

Most part-time real estate assistants work 20 to 24 hours a week, while full-timers are in the office for 35 to 40 hours, Monday through Friday. Weekend work is common, because real estate is a seven-day-a-week industry.

A part-time assistant who works fewer than 20 hours a week will find it difficult to be an effective member of the agent's team. Part-timers should be at the office every day: while personal accommodations can often be made, the assistant should work for the business, not expect the business to work for the assistant.

Some real estate assistants combine aspects of full- and part-time employment by being **on-call**. These assistants essentially mimic the professional behavior and schedule of the agent, working nights and weekends up to 50 or 70 hours a week (or more). As licensed assistants, they show homes, attend closings, measure properties and assist in negotiations. In return, they receive a salary plus commission and the satisfaction of having considerable responsibility for the office's volume and growth.

THE REAL ESTATE ASSISTANT'S CAREER PATH

Most assistants begin their careers as the main or only assistant to one agent. Even if this is just part time, the demands of the job will require the assistant to be able to perform a wide variety of duties that require different types of training and expertise: computer skills, phone skills, marketing and real estate law are just some of the areas in which a real estate assistant must become proficient. In the late 1980s, it was common for agents to hire non-licensed real estate secretaries to perform administrative duties. Today, many agents feel the need to have licensed assistants who participate actively in sales and marketing. Individuals who have not kept up with the changing demands of the marketplace are being phased out, even though their limited skills were perfectly satisfactory just a short time ago.

Once an assistant has gained experience, it is possible to move from the jack-of-all-trades role into a more focused job description, especially in larger real estate firms where specialization is more convenient than in smaller team environments. It's a good idea to be aware of all the possible areas of specialization, even if only to understand the kinds of skills required of the general assistant.

Unlicensed Real Estate Assistants

As discussed earlier in this chapter, unlicensed assistants are generally restricted to administrative and secretarial functions, out of the mainstream of real estate transactions. A motivated and trained **administrative assistant** or **real estate secretary**, however, performs important functions in keeping a real estate office running smoothly. They often acquire valuable skills and knowledge vital to the office's effectiveness.

A **closing coordinator** (also known as a **conveyancer**), however, does not need a real estate license to follow all files from the time the purchase agreement is written until the closing is complete. The closing coordinator makes sure that all the necessary documents are included with the transaction file, and that all files and forms are distributed to the right people. Many unlicensed real estate assistants move into closing coordinator positions.

Unlicensed assistants may also become **telemarketing assistants**, hired by the agent to prospect for business over the phone. However, an unlicensed assistant's ability to solicit listing presentations for the agent may be restricted by state law.

Licensed Real Estate Assistants

A variety of career paths are open to experienced, licensed real estate assistants.

A **marketing assistant** or **marketing coordinator** is responsible for marketing both real estate and the agent. In smaller businesses, he or she will design and produce advertisements, home brochures, home marketing booklets and informational flyers that feature the agent's experience and skill. In larger offices, the marketing coordinator will be in charge of creating and budgeting new marketing programs, running weekly marketing sessions and designing new products.

Most **listing coordinators** are licensed real estate assistants. They take responsibility for files from the time the property is listed until its sale closes, and are completely in charge of scheduling and arranging sales activities.

Buying assistants work with buyers, helping them understand the financial requirements of home ownership, assisting them in selecting neighborhoods and facilitating mortgage applications. A buying assistant will coordinate showings as well, and may work on his or her own as an agent.

Finally, an **apprentice** is a real estate licensee who has *his or her own office*, but who shares listings, buyers and services with an agent for a specific period of time — usually less than a year. The agent usually receives a portion or percentage of the transaction in return for providing expertise. Similarly, an **intern** is a licensed individual who works as an assistant *in an agent's office* under a contractual agreement for a certain period (usually one to three years). The intern's contract often includes a **noncompetition clause**, under which he or she agrees to practice real estate in a different area once the term is up. Both apprentices and interns represent transitional phases for real estate assistants: they are people who plan to become sales agents once their training is complete.

INTO THE FUTURE

As we move toward the 21st century, it is becoming clear that the real estate assistant's role is rapidly evolving. From its office manager origins in the 1980s, the real estate assistant has become an active, licensed member of the real estate agent's team in less than 15 years. Over the next decade, it looks as if the assistant will become more and more a licensed business manager, taking over virtually all of the agent's non-sales responsibilities and freeing real estate agents to do what they do best. That will mean extensive technical and professional training for assistants in changing fields such as electronic communications, marketing theory and graphic design.

SUMMARY

Real estate assistants first appeared in the real estate industry in the late 1980s. Today, nearly all the top real estate firms employ real estate assistants, and ten percent of all sales associates have assistants.

State real estate laws regulate the types of activities in which real estate assistants are permitted to engage. Unlicensed assistants are generally limited to clerical and office management functions, while licensed assistants are permitted to participate in all aspects of the real estate business.

Real estate assistants may be employees or independent contractors, depending on the degree of control their employer exercises over their day-to-day activities. In addition, assistants may work full-time, part-time or be on-call.

Most assistants begin their career as the main or only assistant to one agent. Over time, and as they gain training and experience, real estate assistants can move into a variety of specializations.

KEY TERMS

administrative assistant
apprentice
buying assistant
closing coordinator
conveyancer
employee
independent contractor
intern
listing coordinator
marketing coordinator
marketing assistant
noncompetition clause
on-call
real estate secretary
telemarketing assistant

Review Questions

1. A real estate agent who employs a real estate assistant is likely to have
   a. the same number of listing presentations as other agents.
   b. fewer listing presentations than other agents.
   c. four times as many listing presentations as other agents.
   d. twice as many listing presentations as other agents.

2. The real estate law of the state of North Fredonia requires that "*any person who is associated with a real estate brokerage firm in any way, and who provides members of the public with any information regarding the location, condition or price of residential housing available for sale, must be duly licensed in accordance with this Act.*" *P* is an unlicensed real estate assistant working for a sales associate at Marx Realty in Fredonia City. If a customer calls looking for a house in the city, which of the following may *P* tell the caller?
   a. The addresses, but not the prices, of her agent's listings in the city
   b. The price of a specific home identified by the caller
   c. Whether the sales associate is available to take the call
   d. Whether the sales associate's listings in the caller's price range have new kitchens and air conditioning

3. Which of the following is an unlicensed real estate assistant generally permitted to do?
   a. Show properties to prospective buyers
   b. Negotiate a sales transaction
   c. Place a "For Sale" sign in a front yard
   d. Answer questions about title issues

4. The activities an unlicensed assistant may legally perform are determined by
   a. the terms of the employment agreement with the agent.
   b. the state's Real Estate Assistant Licensing Act.
   c. the federal real estate license laws.
   d. state real estate laws and the office policy

5. A person who works regular hours under the direct control of an employer is probably a(n)
   a. independent contractor.
   b. employee.
   c. apprentice.
   d. part-timer.

6. An independent contractor is entitled to
   a. do his or her job with little supervision.
   b. two weeks of vacation every year.
   c. have taxes withheld from his or her pay.
   d. a regular weekly salary.

7. A real estate assistant who works on an "on call" basis is
   a. unlikely to work evenings and weekends.
   b. most likely to work a 20-hour week.
   c. on the same schedule as an agent.
   d. probably not a real estate licensee.

8. A licensed real estate assistant is *least* likely to move up in his or her career into a specialized field such as
   a. marketing coordinator.
   b. telemarketing assistant.
   c. buying assistant.
   d. intern.

Professional Assistants in the Real Estate Office

In this chapter, we will more closely examine the environment in which the real estate assistant works on a day-to-day basis. By the end of the chapter, you should be able to recognize the basic business structures in which a real estate assistant works.

We will consider the actual tasks that an agent is likely to delegate to his or her assistant. By the end of the chapter, you should be able to identify the five areas of delegated responsibility.

We will introduce the real estate assistant's various functions in the office, and discuss how each is carried out. By the end of the chapter, you should have a clear idea of exactly what a real estate assistant does in the typical real estate office.

WHY DO AGENTS NEED ASSISTANTS?

Every real estate agent is his or her own small business. Even the largest real estate firms, with hundreds of agents and multiple offices scattered all over a city or region, is made up of a collection of small, independent businesses. Each agent is responsible for running his or her business just as if he or she were a doctor, lawyer or shopkeeper. And in addition to the main focus of the agent's business — moving real estate from sellers to buyers — there is a huge volume of paper work to be dealt with, customer service issues to be addressed and other necessary but time-consuming tasks that distract the agent's attention from keeping his or her business alive. The more time an agent spends keeping the files current, making phone calls, prospecting for listings and otherwise taking care of things in the office, the less time he or she will have to be out with buyers and sellers. And being out with buyers and sellers is how a real estate agent makes money. If the agent does not have a real estate assistant to keep things going on the inside, the agent can't be outside.

An agent who doesn't have an assistant is not just a full-time agent: he or she is a full-time agent *and* a full-time assistant, and there are only 24 hours in a day — even a real estate agent's day. As anyone who has ever held down more than one job at the same time knows, it is a highly stressful situation that can have a dismal effect on your mood, your family life and your ability to meet your other goals. When you're tired, distracted and under stress, it is often difficult to do either job as well as you'd like to. It's the same situation for the real estate agent without an assistant.

The first priority of a good real estate agent is to be free to do what will produce income: working with buyers and sellers. However, because they are entrepreneurs, each running his or her own small business and each having an emotional and financial stake in its success, agents tend to be "control freaks" — they have to be the first and last person to touch everything. Usually, it's only exhaustion and the sheer desperation to become more productive that drives them to finally give up some control to an assistant.

I became an agent in 1979. By 1986, I was a top producer in my state, but I was stuck. I knew I could generate more sales volume, I had a burning desire to be number one, but where was the time? Then my husband decided our marriage was over, leaving me with three small children and our newly constructed dream house. I knew had to double my income, so I hired my first assistant, a single mom looking for a flexible job. Things just took off from there.

WHEN DO AGENTS NEED ASSISTANTS?

Typically, agents need real estate assistants when their professional careers reach one of four turning points:

- ❖ When they achieve in excess of $3 million a year in sales
- ❖ When they average more than four to six sales every month
- ❖ When they decide it's time to actively market themselves
- ❖ When they want to break through the production barrier and create a "mega-business"

Only if an assistant takes over certain important but time-consuming tasks can the agent focus his or her attention on growing or maintaining a thriving real estate business.

DELEGATION OF RESPONSIBILITY

Many brilliant sales agents do not have the time (or inclination) to delegate or prioritize tasks. They are successful in their field because they are goal-oriented, highly focused, energetic and interested in all aspects of their profession. They are highly social, and often perfectionists. Unfortunately, those characteristics, while vital to the agent's success, are not the kinds of characteristics found in people who find it easy to delegate responsibility to others.

Even if they do manage to delegate authority to an assistant, agents know the results they want, but often don't have time to give detailed orders or lay out plans. A good assistant is one who can contribute to the team's success by making decisions and carrying them out independently.

There are five essential parts of any real estate office's business structure. In order of priority for the real estate agent, they are:

1. Sales
2. Marketing and Prospecting
3. Administration
4. Production
5. Fieldwork

Sales obviously includes listing and selling property. It's where the commissions come from, and so it is the top priority. If there are no sales, there won't be any need for an assistant: there will be no real estate office. Selling includes showing properties to prospective buyers. **Marketing** is how sales are obtained. It includes advertising properties as well as advertising the office. Marketing also includes promoting the agent personally — ensuring that his or her name is out in the marketplace, that potential buyers and sellers will think of him or her when they decide it's time to buy or sell. **Prospecting** refers to finding new customers, clients and properties to be the targets of marketing and sales efforts.

Administration is the inside work that supports both sales and marketing. Administration includes processing all the paperwork a real estate agent generates, from listings and purchase agreements to closing documents and personnel files. Rent must be paid for the office space, payroll processed for employees, mail needs to be distributed and letters need to go out. Bills must be processed and paid for office supplies and equipment. The agent's schedule must be kept up to date, and the calendar must reflect the most current information available. **Production** is the completion or assembly of particular projects, from having new business cards printed to generating home brochures and advertising flyers.

Fieldwork is a broad category that includes everything else. Fieldwork involves running errands, addressing emergencies, and going outside the office to put up signs, deliver keys and sit at open houses. If it's outside the office door, it's fieldwork. Fieldwork also includes such unlicensed in-office functions as general trouble-shooting, clean-up and assisting other agents with general office work.

The agent is most likely to delegate responsibility in the reverse order of importance. That is, a real estate assistant will probably be assigned tasks as follows:

1. Fieldwork
2. Production
3. Administration
4. Marketing and Prospecting
5. Sales

Only a licensed assistant will be permitted to perform sales-related jobs. In addition, state real estate laws may limit the kinds of marketing activities an unlicensed assistant will be able to do.

The Real Estate Assistant's Role

In Chapter 2, we outlined several types of job descriptions relevant to real estate assistants, such as marketing coordinator and telemarketer. Figure 3.1 shows where they fall in the structure of the real estate office.

Real estate agents do not have time to conduct extensive training seminars for their assistants, and would prefer to have an assistant who is familiar with the industry and the demands of the job, who is able to hit the ground running and take over a number of aspects of the business with a minimum of get-acquainted time.

In any real estate office, there will be a number of expectations about the real estate assistant's performance and presence on the job. The following are typical characteristics agents expect of first-rate assistants:

- ***Discretion*** — The assistant is going to be exposed to clients' personal and financial information: can he or she be counted on to ensure that private documents and confidential communications remain private and confidential?
- ***Organization*** — The assistant is being hired to help keep paperwork and details from becoming confused or overwhelming the agent's ability to practice real estate: can he or she establish a schedule and stick to it?
- ***Observation*** — The agent will not want to have to repeat instructions: can the assistant pay attention and remember details? Can the assistant learn quickly to anticipate what the agent will need and want?

Figure 3.1 The Real Estate Assistant in the Real Estate Office

FIELD WORK	PRODUCTION	ADMINISTRATION	MARKETING	SALES
field coordinator	marketing assistant	office manager	marketing assistant	listing coordinator
	closing coordinator	business manager	call coordinator	buying assistant
		administrative assistant/secretary	telemarketer	

- ❖ ***Appearance*** — In a highly public profession, appearance matters: can the assistant be trusted to dress and speak professionally, to be a positive representative of the agent and the company both in and out of the office?

- ❖ ***Courtesy*** — The assistant is often a potential client or customer's first point of contact with the agent: can the assistant be counted on to use a professional and courteous tone in telephone conversations, to take accurate messages and ensure they're delivered, and to help visitors develop a positive attitude about the agent and the office? Every voice mail message, every letter, is an extension of the agent, and is taken by the community as evidence of his or her professionalism.

- ❖ ***Honesty*** — Clients and customers will not necessarily distinguish between the assistant and the agent when it comes to having their questions answered: will the assistant be tempted to lie or guess if he or she doesn't know the answer to a question? "I don't know, but let me find out for you" never got anyone sued.

- ❖ ***Attention to Detail*** — The assistant will be dealing with important legal documents and other papers that require truth and accuracy: can the assistant be trusted to check and double-check all documents for typographical errors and mistakes?

- ❖ ***Personality*** — The real estate business is fast-paced and busy, with sometimes stressful conditions and last-minute demands on an assistant's time: is the assistant motivated, enthusiastic and able to handle stress? Does he or she have a positive attitude and willingness to work hard? A sense of humor is important, but can the assistant be counted on to be serious, too?

- ❖ ***Independence*** — The agent is hiring an assistant so he or she can do other work: is the assistant a self-starter, able to take charge and handle situations as they arise without always running back to the agent for advice? On the other hand, can the assistant be trusted to ask for advice when he or she really needs it? Does the assistant demonstrate initiative? Does he or she come up with ideas to make the office more efficient or economical? Can he or she still be a team player?

- ❖ ***Training*** — The agent will be expecting a base of expertise and skill: is the assistant computer-literate? Can he or she use a word processor, spreadsheet and desktop publishing program efficiently and accurately? Is he or she familiar with the most current office technology, as well as the standard equipment? Are his or her mathematical abilities and language skills, both written and oral, at an appropriate professional level? Does the assistant have a basic understanding of the real estate industry, its law and practice?

- ❖ ***Dedication*** — Does the assistant demonstrate professionalism and a dedication to his or her career? Does he or she keep informed about current developments and opportunities that will help the agent as well as the assistant? Is the assistant's loyalty obvious?

These factors are very important: they are the generic job description for the real estate assistant. Of course, before you can be hired, you have to be interviewed for the position. At the end of this chapter, in Figures 3.3 through 3.9, we've provided you with a preview of what you might expect from a job interview for a real estate assistant position. The examples include a list of what agents look for in a real estate assistant's résumé; sample interview questions (for both first and second interviews); and basic skills, spelling, math and proofreading tests actually used by many agents. If you can respond to the interview questions intelligently and answer the tests correctly, you should have little trouble finding a rewarding position as a real estate assistant.

WHAT REAL ESTATE ASSISTANTS DO

In Chapter 2, we discussed the findings of a National Association of REALTORS® survey about real estate assistants. The survey included questions regarding the kinds of work assistants were expected to perform.

According to the NAR survey, assistants spend most of their time on the following tasks:

- ❖ Scheduling listings and preparing documents
- ❖ Developing marketing tools
- ❖ Meeting with appraisers, inspectors and lenders
- ❖ Adding listing entries to multiple listing services
- ❖ Acting as office receptionist
- ❖ Prospecting
- ❖ Attending open houses
- ❖ Telemarketing
- ❖ Attending closings or escrows

As you can see, a real estate assistant's responsibilities cover virtually all aspects of the real estate business. That's why training and education are so vitally important to an assistant's successful career.

The National Organization of Real Estate Assistants (NORA) trains both real estate assistants and real estate agents. Assistants (and prospective assistants) can receive broad-based professional career training from NORA, which offers the designation of Accredited Residential Assistant (ARA). Agents receive training and counseling on the effective use of a real estate assistant. Career training and certification is also available from a variety of other professional and educational organizations, including affiliates of the National Association of REALTORS® and colleges or career centers.

Where They Do It

In Figure 3.2 you'll see a floor plan of a suburban real estate office. While the office where you end up working may be larger or smaller, real estate offices usually have the same sort of basic layout and features.

The office in Figure 3.2 has a large reception area with two big windows (one to the right of the doors and the other on the left wall) where photographs of featured listings may be displayed. There is a formal station for the receptionist, large enough for two or even three people to be working there at the same time. Behind the receptionist's workstation is a small meeting room, which might be used for looking at MLS books with prospective buyers, for example, or for writing up offers to purchase. The computer room and file room are connected for convenience. The computer room would have one or more computer workstations (depending on the number of agents), printers, photocopiers and the fax machine. There might also be a vending machine and certainly a coffee maker. The agents' desks are in a large, central area: this is also the area in which an assistant's desk might be located, although a workstation in the file and computer area is just as likely. The broker has a private office, and there is a large conference room for meetings, closings and continuing education.

Figure 3.2 Real Estate Office Floor Plan

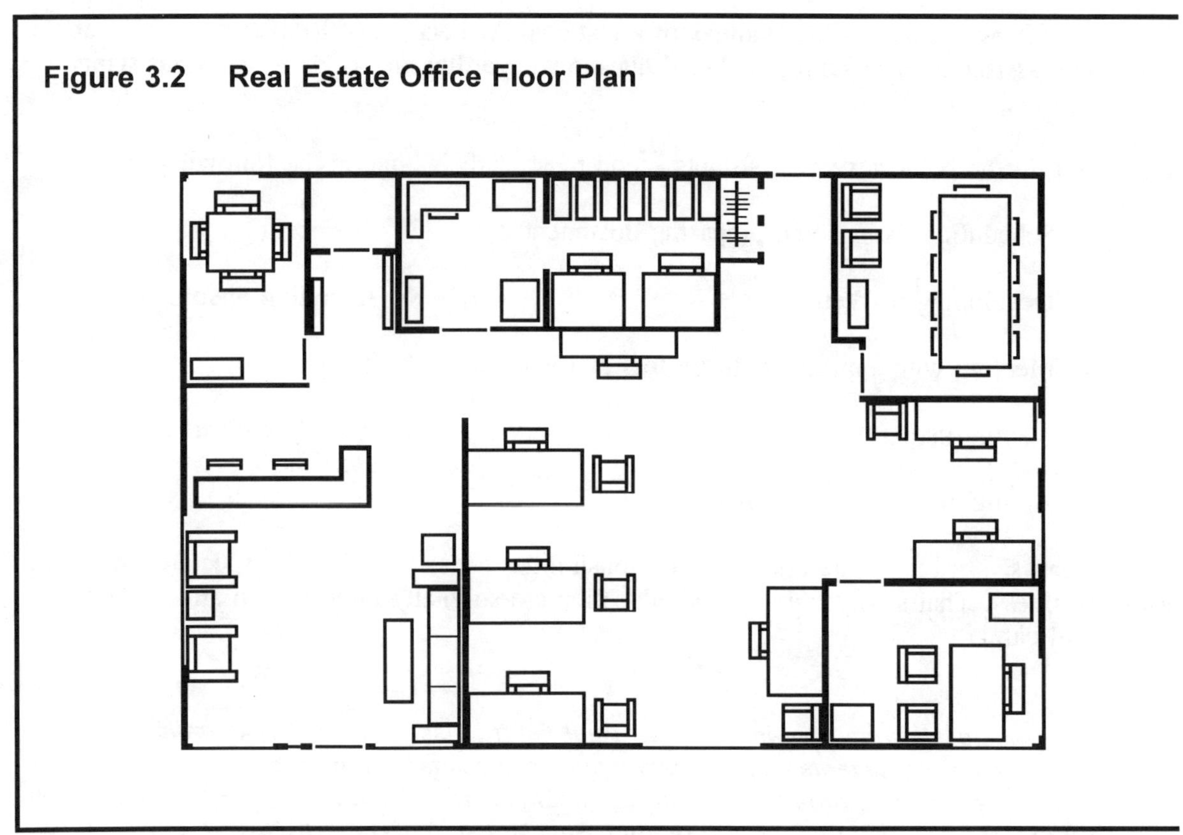

Figure 3.3 What Makes a Good Real Estate Assistant Résumé?

1. *Consistent Job Flow*	An agent doesn't want a "job jumper" who changes employers every six months.
2. *Customer Service Background*	An agent wants someone with good people skills and interpersonal experience.
3. *Real Estate Background*	Someone already familiar with the industry brings with them a basic knowledge of real estate transactions. That can save the agent some training time.
4. *Educational Background*	While education should not be the only consideration, it may give the agent an idea of the applicant's motivation for self-advancement.
5. *Specific Job Skills and Training*	A variety of skills (such as computer, typing and dictation) is a good indicator of whether an applicant is easy to cross-train, and his or her ability to pick up new skills.
6. *Recommendations*	This can be a big plus. An evaluation of the applicant's work from a former employer is an extremely valuable item for an agent.
7. *Professional Presentation*	The agent will look for well-written sentences, no typos, and correct punctuation. The résumé's general layout and appearance is very important, too, because it demonstrates what the applicant considers to be an attractive final written product.
8. *Something Personal*	Include some distinctive information that will make the agent want to know more about you.

Figure 3.4 Sample Interview Questions: First Interview

1. Why are you considering giving up your current job or position?
2. What exactly did you do at your last job?
3. In your last job, what was your workday like? What were your responsibilities?
4. If you had more spare time, what would you do with it?
5. What accomplishments are you most proud of professionally? Personally?
6. How would you handle a customer who was upset about something the agent hadn't delivered? Could you turn that situation around?
7. How would you handle a customer who called and was angry?
8. When, during the day, do you tend to dig into the tough problems? Why?
9. How many tasks can you handle at once?
10. How do you organize your work?
11. What kind of people annoy you?
12. Tell me about the worst supervisor you ever worked for.
13. Tell me how you handled working in that situation.
14. What decisions did you make in your last job?
15. Have you had problems working with others?
16. What experience have you had in real estate? Have you ever purchased or sold a home or handled rentals?
17. What aspects of working in a real estate office interest you?
18. What do you hope to be doing two years from now? How much do you want to be earning?
19. Tell me about your biggest frustrations in your business/working career.
20. What has been your most rewarding work-related experience?
21. What are your career goals?
22. If anything would take you away from work, what would it be?
23. Do you have reliable transportation?
24. Do you listen to instructional tapes or attend seminars?
25. How fast do you type? May I test you?
26. What computer skills do you have?
27. Have you driven around our area? Can you find a specific neighborhood?
28. Do you have a real estate license? Have you ever been a real estate agent?
29. Have you worked in escrow?
30. Have you taken any courses regarding title insurance, or worked in the title insurance field?
31. Have you taken any time management courses or training?
32. Do you use a daily planner?
33. Have you had extensive experience with over-the-phone client service?
34. What does "client for life" mean to you?

Figure 3.5 Sample Interview Questions: Second Interview

1. Where do you hope to be in five years?
2. What do you think it takes to be a successful real estate agent?
3. Have you ever worked with an agent before?
4. When were you *least* motivated?
5. How do you schedule your time?
6. How do you set priorities and solve problems of conflicting priorities?
7. How long would you be interested in holding a position such as this?
8. What is your greatest strength?
9. What do you consider to be your greatest weakness?
10. Describe the worst day on your last job. How did you handle it?

Figure 3.6 Capitalization and Salutation Test

Please read the directions and complete each section as indicated.

Capitalization: *Circle each letter or would that you feel should be capitalized.*

mr. jones	navy blue
the midwest	gulf of mexico
chicago	uncle david
economics	helen thomas
the bright sun	north dakota
the new york times	pepsi cola
united kingdom	economics 101

Salutations: *Please provide the correct salutation for a business letter.*

Example: *James Monroe*	*Salutation: Dear Mr. Monroe:*
Mr. Leo Lion and Mr. Thomas Caton	*Salutation:*
Susan Smith	*Salutation:*
Mr. Steve Hawking and Ms. Maria Nelson	*Salutation:*
Mr. and Mrs. Scott Smith	*Salutation:*
Helen Brown, M.D.	*Salutation:*
Dr. Gerald Thomas	*Salutation:*
Dr. Mary Smith and her husband, Bob	*Salutation:*
The wife of Dr. Irving Zack	*Salutation:*

Figure 3.7 Spelling and Alphabetizing Test

Spelling. *Circle the words that are misspelled.*

absence	eminant	mispelled	sieze
analasis	extrememly	ommision	seperate
bookeeper	flexible	persistant	tangable
changeble	guarantee	practically	termperary
competant	illegall	rational	until
decision	leisur	recommend	vicious
defer	miscellaneus		

Alphabetizing. *Please alphabetize the lists below.*

1. McLaughlin, Meier, Morgan, MacDonald, Miller.

    1.
    2.
    3.
    4.
    5.

2. Yaeger, Boeder, Girelle, Johnson, Kline, Wilson, Thomas, Egert, Nixon, Reynolds.

    1.
    2.
    3.
    4.
    5.
    6.
    7.
    8.
    9.
    10.

Figure 3.8 Math Test

1. Walter just sold a house for $329,000. He was paid a 7 percent commission. How much was Walter paid?

   Answer: ______________

2. Wanda just listed an apartment building for $3.7 million. Please write that numerically.

   Answer: ______________

3. Please add these figures: $4.17; $1,322.91; $482.29; $615.01; $22,400.89.

   Answer: ______________

4. Please subtract $89.03 and $134.26 from the answer to question number 3.

   Answer: ______________

5. What is: (A) 92 ÷ 6 (B) 172 ÷ 11 (C) 19 ÷ 182 ?

   Answers: (A) _________ (B) _________ (C) _________

Figure 3.9 Proofreading Test

Please correct any errors in the following letter.

January 10, 1996

Mr. Mike jones
234 Apple way
Long Beach, Ca 90807

Dear Mr jones,

Enclosed is your closing statement for this past yera. In all the confusion of a real estate transaction, this paperwork is probably not easily accessible for you. I thought I would help by providing yu with this document.

As you know,this will be one of the first documents that your accountant need.By providing you with this serviec, I hop I am releiving one of the small details that seem so plentiful during tax time.

Please have yuou accountant call me if he or she has any questions. In adition, if I can offer any further assistance, perwork, or real estate advisee, please call.

It is my goal to have you and your family as client for life.

Answers to Figures 3.6 through 3.9

3.6 Capitalization and Salutation Test

Mr. Jones	navy blue	Dear Mr. Lion and Mr. Caton:
the Midwest	Gulf of Mexico	Dear Ms. Smith:
Chicago	Uncle David	Dear Mr. Hawkins and Ms. Nelson:
economics	Helen Thomas	Dear Mr. and Mrs. Smith:
the bright sun	North Dakota	Dear Dr. Brown:
The New York Times	Pepsi Cola	Dear Dr. Thomas:
United Kingdom	Economics 101	Dear Dr. and Mr. Smith:
		Dear Mrs. Zack:

3.7 Spelling and Alphabetizing Test

absence	✓eminent	✓misspelled	✓seize	defer
✓analysis	✓extremely	✓omission	✓separate	✓miscellaneous
✓bookkeeper	flexible	✓persistent	✓tangible	
✓changeable	guarantee	practically	✓temporary	
✓competent	✓illegal	rational	until	
decision	✓leisure	recommend	vicious	

1. MacDonald; 2. McLaughlin; 3. Meier; 4. Miller; 5. Morgan

1. Boeder; 2. Egert; 3. Girelle; 4. Johnson; 5. Kline;
6. Nixon; 7. Reynolds; 8. Thomas; 9. Wilson; 10. Yeager

3.8 Math Test 1. $23,030 2. $3,700,000 3. $24,825.27
4. $24,601.98 5. A = 15.33 B = 15.64 C = 0.104

3.9 Proofreading Test

January 10, 1996

Mr. Mike Jones
234 Apple Way
Long Beach, **California** 90807

Dear Mr. Jones:

Enclosed is your closing statement for this past **year**. In all the confusion of a real estate transaction, this paperwork is probably not easily accessible for you. I thought I would help by providing **you** with this document.

As you know, this will be one of the first documents that your accountant **will** need. By providing you with this **service**, I **hope** I am **relieving** one of the small details that seem so plentiful during tax time.

Please have **your** accountant call me if **he or she** has any questions. In **addition**, if I can offer any further assistance, **paperwork** or real estate **advice**, please don't hesitate to call.

It is my goal to have you and your family as **clients** for life.

SUMMARY

Every real estate agent is his or her own small business. Agents typically need real estate assistants at one of four turning points in their careers. Only if an assistant takes over certain important but time-consuming tasks can the agent focus his or her attention on growing or maintaining a thriving real estate business, but it is often difficult for effective real estate agents to delegate responsibility.

There are five essential parts of any real estate business: sales, marketing, administration, production and fieldwork. Only a licensed real estate assistant will be able to perform sales-related jobs; state real estate laws may further limit the kinds of marketing activities an assistant may engage in.

In any real estate office, the agent expects certain characteristics of a first-rate assistant: discretion, organization, observation, appearance, courtesy, honesty, attention to detail, personality, independence, training and dedication. Those factors outline the basic job description of a real estate assistant.

Real estate assistants and can receive basic and continuing professional education from the National Organization of Real Estate Assistants (NORA) and other educational organizations. NORA offers the ARA designation as evidence of having completed its broad-based training program.

KEY TERMS

administration
fieldwork
marketing
production
prospecting
sales

Review Questions

1. A real estate agent's time is most profitably spent

   a. keeping files current.
   b. making phone calls to potential clients.
   c. working with buyers and sellers.
   d. training a real estate assistant.

2. Which of the following is *not* a time when an agent is most likely to hire an assistant?

   a. When they decide to actively market themselves
   b. When they average more than four to six sales a month
   c. When they make more than $3 million a year in sales
   d. When they first start out in the business

3. The *first priority* in any real estate office is

   a. office administration.
   b. sales.
   c. fieldwork.
   d. marketing.

4. The method in which sales are obtained is

   a. fieldwork.
   b. marketing.
   c. administration.
   d. delegation.

5. Inside work that supports sales and marketing functions in a real estate office is called

   a. fieldwork.
   b. administration.
   c. delegation.
   d. training.

6. Sales-related jobs may be performed by a/an

   a. unlicensed real estate assistant.
   b. licensed real estate assistant.
   c. unlicensed real estate assistant if under supervision of an agent.
   d. licensed real estate salesperson, but not by a licensed real estate assistant.

7. Real estate assistant *R* saw a well-known client's income tax return in a folder in the real estate office. He mailed a copy to his cousin. *R* has failed to exhibit which characteristic of a first-rate assistant?

   a. Organization
   b. Discretion
   c. Independence
   d. Attention to detail

8. Agent *M* told real estate assistant *Q* to deliver some documents to a buyer, then drop off a spare set of keys with a client, then put up a "For Sale" sign in a yard, and then come back to the office. *Q* delivered the documents, dropped off the keys, put up the sign, and went home for supper. Which characteristic of a first-rate assistant did *Q not* exhibit?

   a. Discretion
   b. Appearance
   c. Observation
   d. Attention to detail

9. Keeping informed about current developments in real estate, and passing the information along to the agent, is a sign of

   a. independence.
   b. observation.
   c. attention to detail.
   d. dedication.

10. The real estate assistant's professional organization is known as

    a. NAR.
    b. ARA.
    c. NORA.
    d. NOPA.

Real Estate Office Technology

In this chapter, we will take a close look at the technology of the real estate business: the computer hardware and software and other electronic equipment that makes real estate offices run smoothly and efficiently.

This chapter is not the same as a computer training course; rather, it is intended to give you a basic idea of the kinds of technology you'll be expected to use as a real estate assistant on the edge of the 21st century. We'll also take a look at some of the more traditional low-tech tools of the real estate office: signs, lockboxes and telephones.

By the end of the chapter, you should have a fundamental understanding of real estate technology. You should be able to identify various types of computers and software, and how they are used in the real estate office. You should be able to explain how various technologies work together, and the most effective uses for them.

REAL ESTATE TECHNOLOGY

Technology simply means the way something is done. The wheel was pretty much the last word in cutting-edge technology for a thousand years of human history. In communications, there are a number of technologies: drums were considered the best long-distance communications devices for a long time; today we have telephones, fax machines, electronic mail and the Internet. Ten years ago, no one had heard much about voice-mail, but today nearly everyone has it. In 1946, the first fully electronic computer, called ENIAC, took up 3,000 square feet, weighed 30 tons and contained 18,000 vacuum tubes. Today, the power of that giant first computer is surpassed by a relatively inexpensive laptop model you can carry in your suitcase. The point is that technology, the way things get done, changes all the time. Someone who learned how to use ENIAC, decided it was great, and refused to learn how to use an IBM PC or Apple Macintosh would not be doing a very productive job in any field today.

In the real estate industry, new technologies are of increasing importance. Real estate agents provide their clients with a service. As with any service, the most important factors are speed and accuracy: both the agent and the client want results quickly, with no mistakes. In real estate, mistakes mean money: personnel time wasted; lawsuit damages or settlements; a damaged reputation and loss of future business. That's one reason why real estate professionals are relying more and more on computers, and a reason why real estate assistants need to keep their technological skills current.

Another reason is speed. Instead of paging through an MLS book the size of a big-city phone directory, real estate agents can find a buyer's dream house by going **on-line**: using a computer to search a data base of listings for those that meet the buyer's specifications takes only seconds.

Finally, there is the unavoidable factor of keeping up with the Joneses. Despite all the cooperation among agents, real estate is a highly competitive field. If Orchard Real Estate has a half-hour of television time on the local public access channel, you can be sure that ABC REALTORS® will have one, too. Imagine the advantage that Red Door Realty would have if it was the only office in town with its own telephone! It's the same way with all new technology.

In Chapter 3, we learned that one of the most important characteristics agents look for in real estate assistants is dedication. One sign of an assistant's dedication is whether he or she keeps up with current technological developments that will help the agent or make the office more time- and money-efficient. By reading newspaper articles and magazines about new technologies, watching for technology stories in real estate publications, and attending seminars and trade fairs, you can stay informed about what new technologies can (and cannot) do for the real estate agent.

There are electronic real estate services available on the Internet and via satellite. Agents carry their own laptop computers and have fax machines in their cars next to their cellular phone. Agents are electronically linked to their offices virtually 24 hours a day through their pagers and computer modems. There are hundreds of new technologies out there. It's up to the real estate assistant to learn the ins and outs of the technologies used in his or her office, to master them and to find new and effective ways to apply them.

COMPUTERS

There's no shortage of computers on the market. IBM, Apple, Packard Bell, Digital and Toshiba are just some of the manufacturers. While there are certainly differences among the competing models, they all share the same basic characteristics. In this chapter, we'll concentrate on the fundamental similarities shared by virtually all the computer systems with which a real estate assistant is likely to come into contact.

A **computer system** is made up of hardware and software. **Hardware** are the physical machines that make up the computer system; **software** are the programs that make the hardware do useful things.

Hardware

Most computer systems are made up of six basic pieces of hardware:

1. monitor
2. disk drive
3. keyboard
4. mouse
5. printer
6. modem

The keyboard and mouse (and sometimes the modem) are called **input devices**, because they are used to put information into the computer's memory. The monitor, printer (and sometimes the modem) are called **output devices**, because they permit the information in the computer's memory to be displayed or communicated by the computer for others to see. The disk drive contains the computer's memory, where information is processed and stored.

Together, these components permit the computer user to do anything from writing letters to contacting other computers all over the world. In the few feet of space taken up by this equipment, an individual can run a real estate business.

Monitor

A computer monitor looks like a television screen. It can be either one color (such as white or green or amber against black) referred to as **monochrome**, or full color.

Disk Drive

Everything a computer does must be represented by numbers. A computer can only do one thing: perform calculations. All the data that is input and output is converted to number values by the computer program, and all the amazing things that the computer does are actually just high-level math. The **disk drive** is where all these calculations are performed. It is where programs are stored and run, and where data is retained in the computer's memory. The more memory a computer has, the more programs it is able to run at the same time and with greater speed.

At a basic level, everything in a computer is reduced to a **bit**: a 1 or 0, on or off designation. A **byte** is a group of 8 bits. Computer memory is usually expressed in **kilobytes** (**KB**), or 1,024 bytes, and **megabytes** (**MB** or "megs"), or 1,048,576 bytes. Few office computers have memories measured in gigabytes (more than 1 billion bytes) or terabytes (more than 1 trillion bytes), but such machines exist.

Another important designation is RAM or ROM. **Random access memory** (**RAM**) refers to the computer's ability to access any randomly selected part of a program in the same amount of time as any other part. **Read-only memory** (**ROM**) is a fixed form of memory: once it is written, it can only be read. A ROM program becomes a built-in part of the computer's memory system.

Printer

A **printer** is a device that converts a computer's electronic language into a form readable by humans. It can print on paper or transparencies, producing **hard copy** that can be carried away. Printer quality is measured in dots-per-inch (DPI) and characters-per-second (CPS). The higher the numbers for both DPI and CPS, the faster and better-quality the printed product will be. Some printers, such as dot matrix printers, can be very fast, but the quality of the printing is not as high as that produced by a slightly slower inkjet printer. Laser printers tend to be both fast and high-quality.

Input Devices: Keyboard and Mouse

There are two main devices used to enter data into a computer, to manipulate data within a computer system and to cause the computer to output information: the keyboard and the mouse. A **keyboard** contains a set of letter, number and character keys similar to those found on a typewriter. It also includes a variety of **command keys** that provide shortcuts for having the printer perform special functions, such as running find-and-replace or spell check programs in a word processor. The keyboard also contains a numeric keypad that can be used as a calculator, and directional arrow keys for positioning the cursor on the monitor screen.

A **mouse** is a small, palm-shaped device attached to the computer with a flexible cable. On the top of the mouse are two large buttons; underneath it is an exposed roller ball. Moving the mouse on a desktop or special tractioned surface (called a **mousepad**) causes thc cursor to move around on the screen. Positioning the cursor over certain words or images of buttons on the screen and pressing one of the buttons (an operation called "point and click") works in the same way as pressing a series of command or function keys. Many computer users prefer to use a mouse due to the hands-on feel and quickness of operations.

There are other input devices that are sometimes used in real estate offices. An **optical scanner** is a machine used to input pictures or words into the computer. The scanner "reads" the image being scanned and converts it into the numeric commands the computer understands. Special software programs can then reconvert the scanned image and display it on the monitor screen. A **stylus** is a pen-like device attached to the computer. When a user "draws" on a special board or the monitor itself, the stylus sends the information to the computer, and the image appears on the screen.

Modem

A **modem** is a shorthand name for a "modulator/demodulator" — essentially a device that permits a computer to be connected to a telephone line. Once a computer is "online," it can be connected to other computers in the same office, across town, or around the world. The quality of a modem is measured by how quickly it transmits data, in bits-per-second (bps). Twenty-eight thousand bps is the speed of the fastest modems currently available. With a modem, a fax machine or laptop computer (see below) can be linked to a cellular phone, giving the agent the ability to send and receive information from anywhere he or she can make a phone call. Cellular phones can be connected directly to an MLS database, giving the agent instant mobile access to available listings: a valuable tool when driving buyers around town. New wireless communications technologies will permit an agent at a conference in Cincinnati to use her laptop computer to read the e-mail messages stored in his or her office computer in Los Angeles without leaving the meeting room.

Laptops and Palmtops

Laptop computers are lightweight, portable and as powerful as the traditional desktop models. Laptops generally weigh about 6 pounds, and have color or monochrome screens. A recent model laptop computer is roughly 10" x 8" x 2" and runs on a rechargeable battery that lasts up to six hours. It weighs less than 5 pounds. A **palmtop computer** is, as its name suggests, even smaller than a laptop: while its memory and performance abilities are limited, these calculator-sized computers are handy for note-taking. Portable computers can be limited, connected by phone line to an office's computer, permitting instant access to the power of a larger machine, while maintaining the convenience of their smaller size.

For users of laptop and palmtop computers, the **notebook printer** is a major convenience. A state-of-the-art printer weighs 2½ pounds and measures 12" x 4" x 2" — considerably smaller than most conventional printers. While notebook printers lack the printing quality available from standard desktop laser printers, their print quality is improving all the time.

Online Services

Agents may subscribe to one or more **online services**, which contain vast, easily-accessed networks and data bases. Users can browse special-interests libraries, or "chat" with celebrities, experts and each other by typing and responding to messages. The online services include America Online (3.2 million subscribers); CompuServe (2.05 million subscribers); and Prodigy (1.7 million subscribers). Microsoft Network is another fast-growing online service, built-in to Microsoft's Windows '95 software.

The National Association of REALTORS® offers its members an online service called *REALTORS® Information Network* (*RIN*). It includes access to property advertisements, MLS services, geographic and demographic information, and discussion and communication features that let REALTORS® share ideas and strategies, as well as other electronic features tailored to the interests of real estate agents.

The Internet

The **Internet** is a network of computers that can be linked almost instantly. As a result, any Internet user can connect with another user's computer, and share or transfer information. The **World Wide Web** is an access system that permits users to move around on the Internet with some degree of efficiency. Users get to the web through one of the online services discussed above. On the web are **web sites**: computers that are linked to the web, and which offer information to users. A **browser** is a system that moves users around in the web — as you can see, there are many levels at work here. But for all its complexity, the Internet permits computer users to share information with each other regardless of their location: no long distance phone charges apply, even if information is shared between users in London and Los Angeles. Users can **download** the information — that is, they can have it transmitted to their own computer's memory, or printed by their own printer — whether it is text, forms, photos or sound.

...FOR EXAMPLE

> G wants information about home insulation. She uses a browser service to get on the Internet, and types "home insulation." She clicks on the *Search* button, and her monitor displays a list of 45 web sites where home insulation is the topic of interest. Some of the sites are in the U.S., some are in Canada and others are in Europe. If G clicks on one of the items, she will be connected to that computer within 30 seconds, and can download the information to her printer.

E-mail. The Internet allows users to send each other electronic mail, or **e-mail**, directly from one computer to another. If you know someone's e-mail address, you can communicate simply by typing what you want to say and then sending your message to the recipient's mailbox. E-mail addresses are somewhat odd-looking combinations of words and symbols. The mailbox for a real estate assistant might be *assist@pa.net*, which is pronounced "assist at P.A. dot net." E-mail may also be sent between computers in an office network.

Home page. Many sales associates and real estate companies are setting up web pages on the Internet. This ensures that their services are advertised to the widest possible range of potential clients. When a user who's thinking about buying a home, for instance, enters "real estate" as a search term, he or she may find a list of several local agents. Clicking to an agent's page will provide the user with biographical information about the agent, the firm's history, or a list of homes available in a certain region. Some home pages include photographs of the property along with descriptions and the agent's name, phone number and e-mail address.

SOFTWARE

As mentioned earlier, **software** is the set of electronic commands that make computer hardware work. Software comes in the form of *floppy disks* (in 3½ or 5¼ inch sizes) or *compact disks* (CDs). There are many different kinds of software: here, we will discuss only some of the most widely used.

Software packages will provide important information about the computer system required to run them: be sure there is sufficient memory in your system and that it is compatible with the software before you buy. For instance, if you have a Macintosh system, don't buy IBM software (unless you have a conversion program); if your software requires 5KB of memory, be sure 5KB are available on your computer. The numbers after a program's name indicate its version: for example, WordPerfect 6.1 (a word processing program) is the sixth edition of WordPerfect, with some corrections and revisions; Quicken 3.0 is the third edition of a financial management program; Paradox 4.5 is the fourth edition, fifth update of the database software. Many computer professionals suggest waiting for the ".1" version of any program to ensure that all the bugs have been worked out.

Operating systems. An **operating system** is the computer's basic "intelligence." It is the program that tells the computer how to operate itself and how to run the other software that a user may load into it. Today, there are three operating systems commonly in use: DOS and Windows for IBM-type computers, and Macintosh System 7.

Word processing. The most often used software for real estate assistants is probably the computer's word processing software. This is the software used to create documents, letters and other communications, including marketing materials. The most popular word processing software programs are WordPerfect, Word and AmiPro, although there are many other programs available

Desktop publishing. Many agents like to send out professional-looking newsletters and other marketing materials. Desktop publishing programs are designed to help users produce high-quality printed material that often looks as good as professionally designed and printed products. Examples of commonly used desktop publishing software include Aldus PageMaker, Ventura Publisher and Framemaker.

Spreadsheets. Financial charts, records and analyses used to have to be calculated by hand — a time-consuming job that was prone to errors. The use of **spreadsheet software** such as Lotus 1-2-3, Quattro Pro or Excel has eliminated that task. Spreadsheet software permits users to enter the important numbers (such as revenues, expenditures or expected earnings); the software performs a variety of calculations, presents the numbers in a meaningful way, and stores them for later use.

Other software. There is a software program for virtually any job a computer can do. There are scheduling and organizational programs that permit users to plan their activities and appointments months in advance; tax programs that will not only calculate an individual's or business's state and federal income taxes, but print the completed forms ready to send to the department of revenue or the IRS. There are graphics programs that turn users into artists; communications software for setting up networks; and software just for generating forms, charts or presentation materials.

Database

While it is one of the real estate agent's most valuable assets, a **database** is simply a collection of information stored in a computer's memory. However, that collection can be anything from a list of client names and addresses to a multiple listing service's library of available properties. The information may be sorted and assembled in many different ways, depending on the user's needs at the moment. For instance, a name-and-address database could be used to send out a mass mailing to all former clients, or a more selective mailing to clients whose homes sold for more than a certain amount. An agent can access a MLS database to find comparable properties by specifying price, size, location and amenities; out of the thousands of homes in the database, the computer will display only those that fit the agent's **search parameters**: the specific characteristics sought in the database.

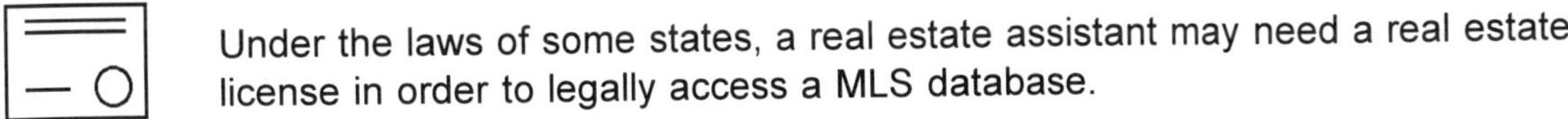

Under the laws of some states, a real estate assistant may need a real estate license in order to legally access a MLS database.

A good database should have the ability to enter, update, search and retrieve client and property records, based on flexible criteria. That is, the computer should ideally be able to display all clients whose middle names end with "t" if (for some reason) the user needs that information. It should be a simple matter to update the database with notes, contact histories and schedules. A good database will be the servant of the user, not require the user to be its servant. Some popular database software specifically for the real estate industry includes OnLine Agent and Top Producer.

...FOR EXAMPLE

M, a real estate agent, has a database that includes all his former clients' names, addresses, phone numbers and home sale information. In addition, each client's file in the database includes the birth dates of their children and spouses, and notes about their jobs, schools and hobbies. When M reads that a local company is moving to another town, he can search the database for all former clients who are employees and send them letters offering his services in selling their homes. He can send birthday cards to clients and family members, and "happy anniversary" notes a year after they've moved into their new house. All of this continuing contact means M keeps his good reputation, gains recurring business from satisfied clients, and often gets new business when clients tell their friends about his good services.

TELEVISION

In many communities, **local access cable** channels provide real estate agents with an effective advertising tool, not only for their services in general, but for specific listings. Homes can be advertised with still photographs as well as video "walk-throughs," and potential buyers and casual browsers can both window shop from the comfort of their homes. If they see a property they like, they can call the agent.

There are an increasing number of real estate-specific television networks. RE/MAX, for instance, has introduced the RE/MAX satellite network (RSN). RSN broadcasts training, educational and motivational programs to an orbiting satellite, which relays the programs to small satellite dishes at network members' offices. Subscribers can watch the programs as they're received, or may videotape them to watch at their convenience.

Videotapes. Videotapes are another television-based medium used by real estate agents. Videotapes can be used "in-house" for training and continuing education, or "outside" to give out-of-town buyers detailed looks at properties, or for consumer education.

In my office, we give our sellers a video called *How To Help Your Agent Sell Your House*. We've found it makes better clients and customers, because they're more informed. They don't worry as much because they know what's going on.

COMMUNICATIONS TECHNOLOGIES

Clear, direct and fast communication is vital in the real estate industry. When someone calls on a listing, the agent wants to be informed. When a buyer is ready to prepare an offer to purchase, the agent wants to know right away. When a seller has finally made up his or her mind, the agent has to know. Certainly, computers are partly a communication tool. We've already seen how they can be networked, linked by e-mail systems and used to access the Internet. Other technologies, however, are specifically designed only as tools to help people communicate.

The Telephone

For all the technology discussed in this chapter, the real estate assistant's most important tool is still the telephone. The computer's link to the virtually infinite information available on the Internet depends on the telephone, but more importantly the telephone is the agent's link to the marketplace. While some potential clients are "surfing the 'net" in search of real estate services, most of a real estate agent's client base comes from phone calls. Those calls may be *outgoing* — part of a telemarketing campaign in which the PA calls potential buyers and sellers to offer the agent's services — or they may be *incoming*: a buyer seeking information about a specific property or a seller who wants a listing presentation. The computer may be an important tool in the real estate industry, but it's still the telephone that drives the office. The next chapter will include a lesson on real estate phone manners, and in chapter 14 we'll examine telemarketing strategies.

Voice Mail

In the old days, if you called someone and he or she was out of the office, the phone would just ring and ring. Or, if the person had a secretary, he or she would answer the call and make a note of your message to give to the person when he or she came back. **Voice mail** is an electronic phone answering system that gives everyone a "secretary" — and much more.

By now, everyone is familiar with voice mail systems. They are used in big companies to route calls to individuals or, if the individual is unavailable, to another appropriate person. The caller becomes his or her own switchboard operator, directing his or her own call by pressing keys on a touch tone phone in response to an interactive recorded message.

Interactive is a word you hear a lot: it means that the system responds to certain actions in a predetermined way. Callers can select the person to whom they wish to speak, or the type of information they need to hear, based on a few simple prerecorded instructions. The call is connected to an agent or another recording, depending on which option is selected. For example, a broker's advertisements might include a reference number for each home. By entering the reference number when instructed to do so by the interactive voice mail system, the caller can hear more information about the property or be connected directly to the listing agent. The system can keep track of how many calls each property receives, which will help the agent know if the ad is effective. By selecting other options, a caller might be connected to a specific agent or the agent on floor duty.

The advantage of voice mail is twofold. First, it ensures that messages are left with the appropriate party. The message is **time-and-date stamped**, which means that when the recording is played back the recipient will know precisely when the call came in. Second, it permits callers to make decisions about their call: do they want to leave a recorded message or do they want to be redirected to someone else? Voice mail messages may be stored indefinitely, although the number of messages that may be kept is limited by the size of an individual's electronic **mailbox** — the computer memory file assigned to each person.

800 numbers. Many agent are discovering the marketing value of having their own toll-free "800" number, either through a service provider or in conjunction with their voice mail. Prospective buyers can call an 800 number listed in an ad or on a sign and enter an extension number that leads them to information on the home in which they're interested. If the caller enters a fax number, he or she can instantly receive an information sheet on the home, as well as any additional information the agent wants to send out. Callers may also elect to be connected with the agent or his or her assistant or pager. In addition, a system with *caller i.d.* will keep a record of callers' telephone number for future telemarketing efforts. Because the number is a free call for the prospective buyer, homes may be effectively publicized on a regional or even national basis.

Cellular Phones

A **cellular phone** is a cordless, portable telephone that uses *cells*, or broadcast areas, instead of wires. Cellular phones have become pocket-sized, and cellular technology is increasing the area over which an agent can be contacted.

Pagers

A **pager** is a small electronic device carried by an agent that keeps him or her in contact with the office. When a call comes in for the agent, he or she can be electronically signaled, even at locations far from the office. Some pagers can be called directly, and display the incoming phone number. Others simply alert the agent to a call, and he or she calls the office to get the message.

Fax Machines

"Facsimile" is simply another word for copy. A **fax** (short for "facsimile") **machine** is a telephone-based system that is capable of sending images over phone lines to another fax machine. The original document is fed into the fax machine and converted into electronic signals. Then the original document is returned to the sender, and the signals are sent over phone lines, just like a phone call, to the fax number (similar to a phone number) entered by the sender. At the destination, the fax machine converts the electronic signals into an image, which is printed.

TOOLS OF THE TRADE

There are a number of low-tech tools that are nonetheless important to real estate agents, such as lock boxes, yard signs and displays. Under the laws of most states, agents must obtain sellers' permission to install lock boxes or to place a sign in front of a property.

Lock Boxes

A **lock box** is a device that is attached to the door of a home, containing the house key. Many agents encourage sellers to permit lock boxes to be installed, because it permits agents to visit the property even when no one is home to make an appointment. The box can only be opened by a member of the local MLS with a key or (in the case of electronic lockboxes) with a coded card similar to an ATM card. A "smart lock box" is a high-tech version of the standard box that keeps a record of which agents visited the home, based on information encoded on their entry cards.

Yard Signs

It's very difficult to sell property if the fact that it's for sale is a secret. Yard signs serve two important functions: first, they let prospective buyers know that the property is being offered for sale; and second, they let prospective buyers *and* sellers know that the listing agent (and his or her office) are active participants in the real estate market.

So yard signs are useful for selling both the property *and* the agent. In some communities, however, yard signs are not permitted. This is often an attempt to avoid "panic selling," where neighbors become worried that the neighborhood may undergo a racial or economic transition, or to control community growth and character. Sometimes sellers prefer not to have a sign, whether because they don't want strangers to know they're moving or don't want other agents dropping by. In any case, not having a yard sign creates a challenging environment for real estate agents.

There are several types of yard signs, ranging from traditional wire-frame metal signs to more sturdy wooden signs. Some agents prefer round signs, others square or rectangular shapes. Some signs have boxes attached to hold flyers about the home. Figure 4.2 illustrates some of the typical styles of yard signs.

Figure 4.2. Yard Signs

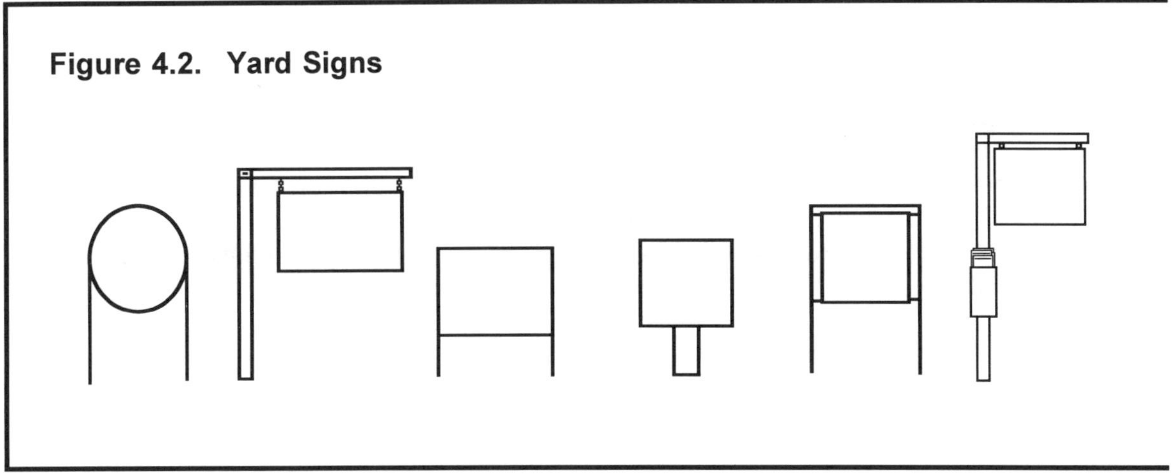

Talking signs contain small radio transmitters and broadcast information about a home's features within a limited area — usually less than 200 feet. The sign itself displays the usual information about the agent and office, along with the radio frequency to which drivers should tune their radios in order to hear more about the home.

Displays

Agents often like to leave printed material about a home in a prominent place, so potential buyers have something tangible to take with them. The materials may simply be left out on a dining room table, or they may be placed in more or less elaborate racks designed to attract attention and make a professional impression. Displays come in metal, cardboard and molded plastic in a wide variety of shapes, sizes and designs.

Promotional Materials

A big part of a real estate agent's business is **self-promotion**: marketing the agent's services and personality to the public. This can be accomplished through the use of postcards, letters and slick brochures. We'll discuss these materials and strategies in Chapter 9. An agent's services may be promoted in newspaper advertisements, on television and on billboards. Many agents prefer to distribute promotional items, too. An agent's name and phone number can be printed on virtually anything, and a number of companies offer personalized promotional items such as refrigerator magnets, coffee mugs and calendars. Promotional items also include housewarming and thank-you gifts to past clients and customers.

There are two main advantages to using promotional gifts. First, they create a positive impression in the marketplace, because people like to receive free things, particularly something useful. Second, an item such as a refrigerator magnet keeps the agent's name prominently displayed in a potential client's home 24 hours a day. A 24-hour television ad would be extremely expensive, with no assurance that anyone would watch.

SUMMARY

A computer system is made up of hardware and software. The monitor is the computer screen, and may be monochrome or color. The disk drivc contains the computer's memory; all the program functions occur here. A printer is a device that converts a computer's electronic language into a human-readable form. Input devices such as a keyboard or mouse allow users to enter commands and data into the computer. A modem is a device that permits a computer to be connected to a telephone line. Through a modem, computer users can be linked into a network or access an online service or the Internet. Laptop and palmtop computers are small but powerful. Software programs are the sets of commands that make computer hardware work.

Local access cable television channels, videotapes and satellite networks provide real estate agents with information, communication and public relations opportunities. The telephone remains the real estate assistant's most important tool. An interactive voice mail system is a convenient and efficient way to direct phone calls and take messages. Cellular phones are cordless, portable phones; pagers can alert agents when they receive a phone message. A fax machine is a telephone-based system that transmits images rather than voices.

A lock box permits members of the local MLS to have access to the key for showings. Yard signs are effective ways to advertise. In the house, agents often use displays to offer brochures and flyers to prospective buyers.

KEY TERMS

bit
browser
byte
cellular phone
command keys
computer system
database
disk drive
download
e-mail
fax machine
hard copy
hardware
home page
input devices
interactive
Internet
keyboard
kilobyte (KB)
laptop computer
local access cable
lock box
mailbox
megabyte (MB)
modem
monitor
monochrome
mouse
mousepad
notebook printer
on-line
online service
operating system
optical scanner
output devices
pager
palmtop computer
printer
RAM/ROM
self-promotion
search parameters
software
spreadsheet
stylus
talking sign
voice mail
word processor
World Wide Web

Review Questions

1. The two basic components of any computer system are the

   a. monitor and printer.
   b. input and output.
   c. hardware and software.
   d. software and data base.

2. Which of the following is *not* an input device?

   a. Keyboard
   b. Mouse
   c. Scanner
   d. Monitor

3. Computer memory may be measured in

   a. kilometers.
   b. megabytes.
   c. trilobites.
   d. modems.

4. *Q*, a real estate assistant, was asked by her agent to select a new printer for the office. The InkZap Printer 2000 (200 DPI; 25 CPS) costs $1,500. The Nicko-900 Printer (450 DPI; 65 CPS) costs $1,600. Which printer should *Q* recommend?

   a. The InkZap, because it has the lowest price.
   b. The InkZap, because it has lower DPI and CPS numbers at a comparable cost.
   c. The Nicko, because it has a higher DPI and CPS numbers at a comparable cost.
   d. The Nicko, because it has a higher price.

5. A computer's basic intelligence is its

   a. operating system.
   b. database.
   c. monitor.
   d. disk drive.

6. *T* types the word "AGENCY" on her computer keyboard, and uses the mouse to point and click on the *search* command. The monitor displays a list of 364 files, including newspaper and magazine articles as well as NAR and state government materials. *T* points and clicks on one of the files, and an article about agency law from the Greater Moscow Association of Land Conveyancers is displayed for *T* to read. What has *T* been using?

   a. The Internet
   b. A modem
   c. A browser
   d. All of the above

7. A real estate assistant's most important tool is probably still the

   a. computer.
   b. laser printer.
   c. telephone.
   d. pager.

8. An interactive electronic phone answering and routing system is also known as

   a. a fax machine.
   b. voice mail.
   c. an online service.
   d. a cellular phone.

9. *H* is selling her home, but she will be out of town for long periods of time. *H*'s agent should encourage her to

   a. have a lock box attached to her door.
   b. wait to list until she will be at home more regularly.
   c. leave a spare key in the mail box.
   d. send keys to all local MLS members.

10. Advertisements, brochures and refrigerator magnets that market an agent's services are referred to as

    a. promotional materials.
    b. displays.
    c. interactive marketing devices.
    d. community access materials.

Professional Skills

I**n this chapter**, we will discuss the professional skills an assistant needs to bring to the real estate office. By the end of the chapter, you should be able to identify the basic skill sets agents require, and the tools and techniques to apply them.

OFFICE ADMINISTRATION

Most assistants begin their careers in the area of **office administration**. By learning how to make an office run more efficiently, the assistant can gain a clearer understanding of its policies and procedures as well as a better idea of how the real estate industry operates.

Every real estate office requires hours of paperwork every week. Developing and applying systems and organizational strategies to this work makes it not only more enjoyable, but also leaves the assistant with more time to spend doing the more interesting parts of his or her job, such as marketing or assisting with sales.

It will typically take an assistant three to six months to become comfortably familiar with all the different documents and papers that flow through a real estate office.

DOCUMENTS AND PAPERWORK

Every real estate agent will have a different idea of how he or she wants papers filed, copied and distributed. However, there are certain basic systems that are the same (or very similar) from office to office. Different kinds of documents require different systems. Local real estate associations will often create standard forms to be used by members.

Listing Papers

One of the most common kinds of forms found in a real estate office are its listing papers. These include the forms required to list a home for sale, forms for reporting the listing to the local MLS, and information sheets that need to be completed prior to a showing.

Generally, an assistant should make sure that the listing papers are signed by the listers (the sellers and the broker). Three copies should be made and distributed to

1. the main office file
2. the listing agent's file
3. the sellers.

Purchase Agreement Documents

The documents that reflect an agreement to buy and sell a property are the legal documents that will be used to transfer ownership. The original and a copy of all purchase agreement documents should be kept in the listing agent's file, and another copy in the main office file. Other copies should be distributed to the buyer, the seller and any cooperating agents. The loan officer and closing or escrow officer will also want their own copies of the purchase agreement papers.

Seller's Statement of Condition or Property Disclosure Reports

In many states, sellers of residential property are required to disclose known defects to potential purchasers. Some states require a general statement of the property's condition; others provide detailed forms that must be filled out by the seller, detailing the condition of the home's major structures and systems. In either case, the document is the seller's declaration of the property's true condition. It is a legally-binding "promise" by the seller that there are no other known defects in the property. A seller may be sued for damages by a buyer who later finds defects that the seller either knew or should have known about. In addition, the real estate laws of most states hold agents liable for a property's condition as well. The agent will be relying on the seller's disclosure statement when he or she answers buyers' questions about the home. In some places, the completed disclosure report must be displayed in full view any time the property is shown.

The original and a copy of the statement should be kept in the agent's file. The assistant will want to prepare multiple copies for distribution at showings. Another copy will need to be delivered to the new buyer. Some states set strict time limits on when this may be done, and allow buyers to cancel a sale if they do not receive a report within the allotted time period.

Other disclosures, such as community code compliance forms, disclosures about well, septic and sewer systems or business relationship disclosures should be copied and kept by the agent.

Change Form

The change form is a universal standard form used whenever any aspect of a listing needs to be changed. A listing agreement is a contract between the seller and the agent, and changes to it must be treated as seriously as changes to any other contract. The change form is a sort of contract-within-a-contract that alters or replaces one or more of the original contract's clauses. For instance, the change form may be used when a seller wants to reduce the asking price or extend the listing period. A change form would also be used if a seller wants to cancel a listing for any reason.

Copies of the change form should be distributed in the same way as copies of the original listing.

Showing Information Form

The showing information form is used to make showings of the property as efficient as possible. The form, filled out by the seller and the agent, establishes the basic policies and procedures of a showing. For instance, the following issues should be addressed:

- ❖ Will a lock box be used?
- ❖ How much notice does the seller need before a showing occurs?
- ❖ Are there pets in the house? Should they be allowed to go out?

All relevant phone numbers should be included, along with any restrictions or special instructions about showings. Copies should be kept by the agent and the information (or a copy) shared with cooperating agents.

Listing Packet

A listing packet is an envelope or file folder that contains all the forms and documents the agent will need to list a home. It should contain a listing form, MLS form, all disclosure forms (both the property condition form and any required agency disclosures) and a showing information sheet. In addition, the packet should include marketing and promotional materials, such as company brochures, and consumer-education materials, such as informational pamphlets published by NAR. The goal of the listing packet is to have all the necessary materials in one convenient place.

A real estate assistant should prepare several listing packets ahead of time, and make sure that there are always at least ten complete packets on file.

Buyer Packet

The buyer packer is similar to the listing packet. It contains the information an agent will want to offer a buyer in order to establish a comfortable relationship. This includes marketing materials about the agent, the broker and the company, as well as such helpful things as maps and other information about schools, recreation and the community in general. The packet should contain a description of the services offered by the agent, and may include agency disclosure materials as well.

A real estate assistant should be sure that there are always ten buyer packets available at any time. You never know when a busload of potential purchasers will come through the door.

Prelisting Packets

Prelisting packets contain the information that is sent out to potential listers before the agent arrives to view the property and make a presentation. The prelisting packet should be sent to the homeowner — mailed, overnighted or hand-delivered by the assistant or a courier service — a few days before the presentation. The packet's content is similar to that of the buyer's packet, plus sample home advertisement layouts and home brochures to demonstrate the kinds of service the seller can expect.

FILE ORGANIZATION

Perhaps the most important question to ask before creating a file or a filing system is: *What do the agent and the company want?* The answer to this question will tell you

- *What* you need to file;
- *Where* the files should be kept;
- *How many* copies of documents you need to make; and
- *Who* should be on the distribution list for files and copies.

The agent's professional focus and the vision or mission statement of the real estate office will give you a good idea about what's important and what procedures are followed to achieve specific goals. Those facts tell you what the paperflow of your office looks like.

A **paperflow** is the way any document — a memo, a phone message, a letter or a listing statement — moves from one person to another in an office. For instance, if the receptionist takes a phone message for an agent, imagine that the message has a long thread attached to it. The trail created by that thread as it unwinds from the receptionist's desk, through the office to the agent's in-box is its paperflow. If the thread crosses anyone else's desk on its way to the agent, then those people are part of the paperflow, and may need copies of documents or access to files. Tracking paperflow is an important first step in deciding how to organize an office's records.

Most agents have some methods of record keeping already in place. Their methods may work well for them — or they may not work so well. In an increasingly competitive environment, it is increasingly difficult for agents to keep up with all the necessary record-keeping and paperwork. That's a big reason why they hire assistants. It's the assistant's job to free the agent from behind the scenes work like keeping records of meetings and transactions, or making the filing system work.

When I came into the agent's office on the first day, I asked what sort of record-keeping system she had. She said, "Oh, I just know where everything is," and pointed to some cardboard boxes filled with papers. The fact is, she *could* find a memo or a phone note if she had to, but sometime it took her hours of rummaging around in those darn boxes! I could really see why she hired an assistant.

File Organization

There are probably as many ways to organize files as there are real estate agents and assistants. Every file clerk since the time of the pharaohs and the ancient Chinese bureaucracy has invented his or her own system for keeping track of where things are. In any office that depends on record-keeping, everyone knows that the person who organizes the files has more real power than the boss. There are, however, some standard filing styles that may be adapted for a particular office's needs.

Alphabetical organization. One of the most common filing systems is the **alphabetical** form. As its name implies, files are organized alphabetically by last name. But whose last name to use? In any real estate transaction, there are at least two major parties — the buyer and the seller. Typically, the files will be arranged according to the last name of the agent's client, whichever party that is. There are, however, two complications. First, the buyer and the seller in a transaction both generate a lot of different information and documents. A single transaction file could easily become very large, especially in a complicated sale. Second, agents need to keep track of both parties for future business opportunities. Keeping all records under a single name may not be the most efficient method for agents who subscribe to the "client for life" theory.

Separate filing. To accommodate this problem, separate files may be kept under the names of the buyer and the seller in a transaction. All the **shared documents** (anything that has both parties' signatures) should go in the client's file. All papers that have to do with only one client — such as internal memos, letters and financing forms — should be kept in the appropriate client's file, with a **cross-reference** to the other party's file. That way, an agent who is interested only in what properties a buyer looked at before finding the home he or she finally bought can look in the buyer's file, and not have to wade through all the transactional documents involving the final sale.

It's a good idea to distinguish client and customer files, too. For instance, if red labels are used on all the seller-client files, and yellow labels are used on all the buyer-customer files, someone looking for a past client can ignore half the folders.

Indexing. Another way to make files more accessible is to create an index. An **index** is simply an alphabetical list of topics (there's an index in the back of this book). An index is particularly useful in a large, high-volume office where there may be many filing cabinets and thousands of files. If the file drawers are numbered, the index can let a searcher know that the "Smith" file is in drawer 35. This method is mostly used where there are multiple files for individual parties: for instance, if there is a "Smith/buyer/1985" file, a "Smith/seller/1990" file and a

"Smith/buyer/1990" file, they may be in different drawers, depending on the system used. An index will tell a user looking for the "Smith/buyer/1990" file exactly where it can be found (See Figure 5.1).

Figure 5.1 Alphabetical Index

This index is arranged alphabetically by last name. The person's status as buyer or seller in a transaction is indicated in boldface if they were a client, italics if not. The address of the property is provided (some filing systems include a separate "Property" file of all the real estate that passes through an office); the date of the transfer, and the drawer number. Each entry includes a cross reference to the other party to the transaction.

SMITH

Jon C. K. and Dr. Paula R.
Buyer — 619 W. Clousterville, 1995: 34
xref: LA MONTAIGNE: 34

SMITH

Thomas V. and Margaret W.
Buyer — 145 Growston, 1990: 16
xref: PURDEY: 14
Seller — 2115 S. Walters 6B, 1990: 19
xref: LAMINSTOGNE: 32
Buyer — 2115 S. Walters 6B, 1985: 8
xref: **SWATCZKAVITZ:** 7

SMARTLEY

Vivian C., *Estate of*
Yolanda T. Guitierrez, *Executor*
Seller — 9 Baltimore Place, 1994: 27
xref: COOPER-FENSTIN: 24

KEEPING RECORDS

No matter what filing system you decide to use, the way you keep records of incoming and outgoing materials is of great importance to how well your filing system works. The way you gather information and keep records determines the usefulness of the materials contained in the files. Imagine that an assistant decided to keep only documents that were printed on blue paper. That would mean that if listing agreements and offers to purchase were printed on white paper, they wouldn't be in the files. On the other hand, what would the files be like if the assistant decided to keep *everything* that came across the agent's desk, including daily newspapers and junk mail? Certainly, nothing important would ever get thrown away, but just imagine the acres of filing cabinets! This illustrates the importance of making sound decisions about what records to keep.

There are two requirements for record-keeping in a real estate office. Agents want their files to be *accurate* and *current*. That means they don't want mistakes or misfilings to mess things up. If files are supposed to be separated into buyer files and seller files, agents don't want to find buyer documents in the seller folder. Agents don't want to have to go looking for a Jon Smith document in the Thomas Smith file. And if the index says a file is in drawer 12, it should be there.

File indexes must be updated on a regular basis: computers make this a simple task. It's a good idea to update the index as soon as a new file is added to the system, rather than occasionally. An agent should be able to rely on the index now.

What to Keep

The records kept should be uniform. For example, in every listing file, there should be certain basic information:

- the address of the property, the owner's name and the year the current owner purchased the property
- the year the property was built and its size in square feet
- the number of rooms, broken down by type
- the price paid for the property by the current owner
- any improvements made by the owner
- the owner's employer, spouse's and children's names and children's ages
- the owner's home and work phone numbers

Each listing file should also include a record of all the agent's or assistant's contacts with the property owner, including post-closing contacts (such as birthday cards or a postcard noting the anniversary of the sale).

If the assistant makes sure that this basic information is contained in each listing file, the agent will know that the file is current. Imagine how embarrassing it would be for an agent to send *two* letters to the same former client! It would not make a good impression. The agent would appear disorganized, and the caring image he or she hoped to project would be erased: it would look to the client as if two copies of an impersonal computer-generated letter had been sent out by mistake, not as if the agent had actually remembered the client. Even if it *is* an impersonal, computer-generated letter sent out automatically on a programmed schedule, appearances are everything: it shouldn't look like a computer sent it.

Details of every listing and sale in your agent's region should be carefully noted, whether or not your agent holds the listing. **FSBOs** (properties that are *F*or *S*ale *B*y *O*wner, pronounced "fizz-boes") should be contacted to find out their asking price and what the property actually sold for. Compiling records of all sales, whether by owner, REALTOR® or independent agent, will help assistants and agents learn more about market activity, hot neighborhoods and other information. Expired listings (available every morning on the MLS computer) should be noted so that they can be called or sent letters of introduction.

Assistants should keep records of all phone calls that came in or went out of the office; letters to and from the agent; and all walk-in activity. A **daily planner** (see Figure 5.2) helps keep track of day-to-day events and responsibilities; an **activity log** (see Figure 5.3) is a tool to organize more long-term projects.

Other records that must be kept include the locations of lock boxes and yard signs. These are usually owned by the agents personally, rather than by the company, so an assistant should be particularly careful that they're not lost. Newspaper advertising deadlines, prices and format requirements also need to be kept on hand for quick reference.

Clipping File

Assistants should keep **clipping files** (also called *morgues*) of important or interesting articles from newspapers, magazines and real estate publications, as well as handouts and materials from professional seminars. Advertisements for the agent's listings, as well as effective ads for other properties, should be clipped and saved for future reference. A clipping file should be organized the same way as any other filing system. Establishing an information and skills library is helpful to agents, who can look up a specific topic in an emergency or browse during "down time."

Keeping a clipping file current is a by-product of the assistant's responsibility to be up-to-date on developments in the real estate industry, technology and law.

Inventory

Equipment and supplies will need to be **inventoried**. That means a record needs to be kept so that supplies can be reordered before the office runs out. No assistant want to leave his or her agent without paper or pens. The assistant will need to know where supplies are purchased and how long it takes to fill an order.

Simply checking the supply cabinet on a regular basis will ensure that no "paper clip emergencies" arise. An effective assistant will not only make sure that the essentials are available, but will try to anticipate the agent's future supply needs. You should also shop around to determine which office supply stores offer the best prices.

Figure 5.2 Daily Planner

MONDAY, JULY 6 188/178	TUESDAY, JULY 7 189/177	WEDNESDAY, JULY 8 190/176
7	7	7
7:15	7:15	7:15
7:30	7:30	7:30
7:45	7:45	7:45
8 *Check Desk for Priorities!*	8 *Check Desk for Priorities!*	8 *Check Desk for Priorities!*
8:15 *Check Voicemail*	8:15 *Check Voicemail*	8:15 *Check Voicemail*
8:30	8:30	8:30
8:45	8:45 *eet with agent*	8:45
9 *Process new Listings*	9	9 *Process new Listings*
9:15	9:15 *Agents Open at Smiths*	9:15
9:30	9:30	9:30 *Deliver lock boxes*
9:45	9:45	9:45 *Press Releases, ads to*
10	10	10 *Town News, Do Banking*
10:15 *Survey Buyers*	10:15	10:15
10:30	10:30	10:30
10:45	10:45	10:45
11 *C As*	11	11
11:15	11:15	11:15
11:30	11:30 *Lunch with Anne*	11:30
11:45	11:45	11:45
12 *Lunch*	12	12 *Office Lunch*
12:15	12:15	12:15
12:30	12:30	12:30
12:45	12:45 *Call Listings*	12:45
1 *Carlson Closing*	1	1 *Call FSBOs*
1:15	1:15	1:15
1:30	1:30 *Call Expireds*	1:30 *Call Expireds*
1:45	1:45	1:45

Figure 5.3 Assistant's Five-Month Activity Chart

ACTIVITY	JANUARY					FEBRUARY					MARCH					APRIL					MAY				
Brochure		X														X									
Market Trends								X										X							
Solicit Listings/Sales			X					X					X					X					X		
Holiday	X																								
Open House																									
Past Clients					X									X											
Survey/Questionnaire					X																				
Just Lstd/Sld/Reduced				X						X			X									X			
Promotional Event								X						X				X			X				
Advertising	X							X																	
Newsletter	X															X									
Press Release											X									X					
Writing			X	X						X		X										X			
Printing								X																	
Follow Up					X											X									
Budgeting								X																	
Vacation/Days Off																X									
Personal/Family																						X			
Seminar/Cont'ing Ed											X	X													

The service dates of equipment such as photocopiers and printers should be recorded so that recurring problems can be pointed out to the repair personnel. All equipment that is under a service agreement should be cleaned and checked regularly: read the agreements and be sure to enforce your right to regular maintenance. Warranty expiration dates should also be noted.

Phone Directory

An effective assistant will keep a Rolodex® or computerized file of important phone numbers, such as:

- listers
- buyers
- past clients
- MLS
- home inspectors
- loan officers
- title companies
- competing brokers and agents
- home and pager numbers of brokers and agents in the office
- newspaper advertising departments
- graphic designers and ad agencies
- photographers
- printers

Other useful numbers that clients, customers and others may need are

- lawn services
- painters
- roofers
- cleaning services
- decorators
- painters
- asbestos removers
- pest control services
- pool cleaners
- utility companies
- cable companies
- schools

Agent's Calendar

One of a real estate agent's most valuable possessions is his or her calendar. An active agent sometimes has hundreds of appointments, meetings, phone calls, letters and events scheduled every week. *It is absolutely vital to the real estate agent's success that his or her calendar be current and accurate.* An agent who shows up late for a listing presentation or who misses a showing is going to lose money. Buyers left cooling their heels in front of a house are not going to have a good impression, and sellers whose phone calls are left unanswered will not be likely prospects in the future.

A real estate assistant's primary responsibility is to ensure that the agent can work without worry. One way this is accomplished is to keep the agent's calendar updated. Important events include such things as

- listing appointments
- showings and open houses
- closings
- contingency deadlines

- listing expiration dates
- walk-throughs
- license renewal
- housing inspections
- appraisals
- education deadlines

Accounting and Bookkeeping

Some agents have their assistants balance their personal and business accounts. Business accounting duties may be a part of an assistant's job description. An assistant whose responsibilities include accounting and bookkeeping functions should keep careful records of all financial transactions in the office: both expenses and income. A file should be kept for copies of the agent's business-expense receipts, which should be organized in a logical fashion, such as by type of expense (food, travel, materials) or activity (sales-related, marketing-related). *Receipts should never be lumped together as "general expenses."*

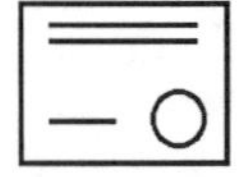

Agents are required to keep separate accounts to hold earnest money deposits. A real estate assistant may need a real estate license in order to handle these accounts. Check your state's real estate law and your agent's office policy.

Accounting and bookkeeping are valuable office skills that require specific training. While a real estate assistant does not need to be a certified public accountant in order to be responsible for an agent's financial matters, it's a good idea to have some professional training or experience in these areas. State and federal tax laws are complex, particularly those regarding the small business, self-employment, personnel, property and independent contractor issues that arise in real estate. Legal counsel may be necessary, and professional tax assistance is recommended. While computer programs are also available to help prepare income tax returns, they do not eliminate the need for sound professional advice.

TELEPHONE SKILLS

As mentioned in Chapter 4, the telephone is the assistant's most important tool. A large part of the real estate business is conducted over the phone: it's how agents stay in touch with clients and prospects, and how they deliver their messages, products and services. For many potential buyers and sellers, their first contact with the agent will be on the phone. When the telephone rings in a real estate office, it's first-impression time. It's up to the agent's real estate assistant to make sure that the first impression is one of friendliness, professionalism and competence. The first ten seconds are crucial: that's just how long it will take for callers to decide that they like your office, or that they think you're all a bunch of jerks.

Of course, for all its usefulness, the telephone can be a major pain, too. The problem is, it rings even when you're busy with something else. When you answer it, someone usually wants you to do something other than what you were doing at the time. In a fast-paced real estate office, a ringing phone can mean opportunity or disaster: but it always means more work. Piled on top of that is the absence of phone etiquette among some callers. People don't call back when you leave a message; they put you on hold for hours on end; they call back repeatedly to make sure their message was delivered. Other times you find yourself playing "phone tag" with an important prospect or nervous client, leaving messages on each other's voice mail until it becomes ridiculous, and you're both out of patience. On top of all that, it's a real estate assistant's job to be the agent's first line of defense. One of the reasons agents hire assistants is to decrease the demands on the agent's time by taking care of phone calls. That means the assistant needs to

- *screen* for calls he or she can handle without the agent;
- determine which messages have *priority*; and
- *follow up* on calls on his or her own initiative.

The following hints and tips are designed to be a hands-on guide to help you deal with the telephone's non-stop demands. The more effective a real estate assistant becomes at fielding phone calls, the more productive he or she can be.

Controlling Phone-Flow

In the same way that every real estate office has its own paperflow, it also has a "phone-flow." That is, there is always a procedure for directing phone calls to the proper person. In Chapter 4 we discussed the concept of interactive voice mail. In offices with fully interactive voice mail, the phone-flow has been analyzed and structured into the voice mail system. In other offices, the flow may look more like the illustration below:

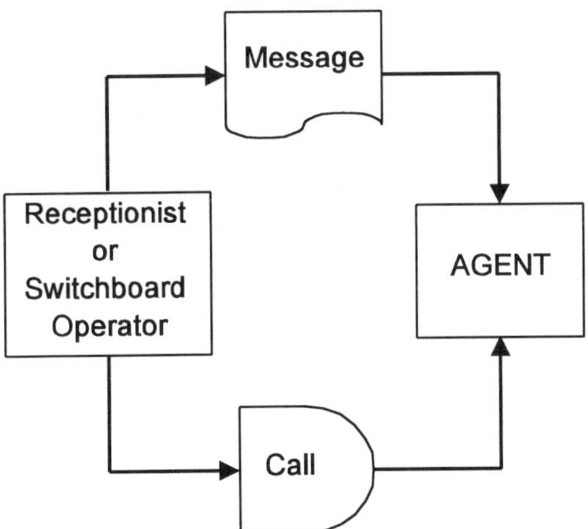

As you can see, either the call or the message go directly to the agent. If the agent gets the call, that means he or she is tied up on the phone and not out with clients. If the message is left on the agent's desk, there's a potential business opportunity just sitting there gathering dust.

With an assistant and a logical, organized system, the phone-flow looks more like the flowchart on the next page.

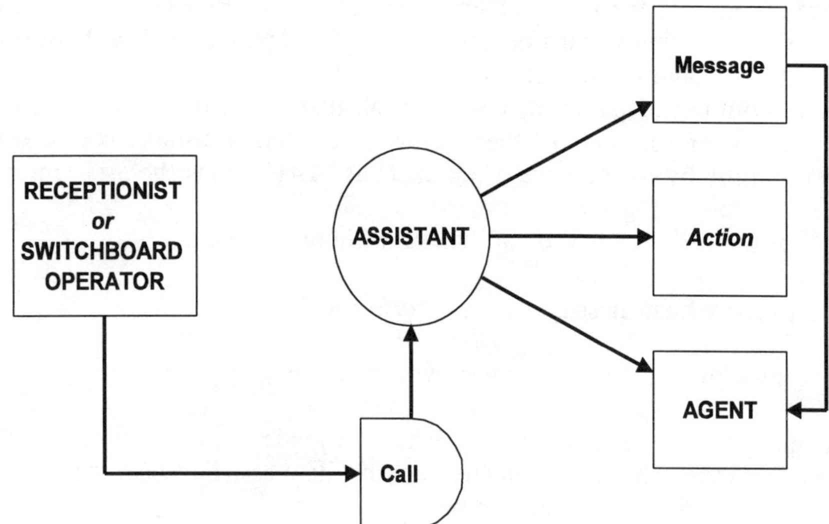

In this system, *all* the agent's calls go through the assistant. That means it's up to the assistant whether to put the call directly through to the agent, to take a message for the agent to look at later, or to take immediate action. While the assistant is fielding phone calls, the agent is freed to conduct a real estate business. The assistant is the agent's shield against time-consuming calls that are better handled by others.

Telephone Answering Techniques

The way the telephone is answered tells callers a lot about the person to whom they're talking. From the way the call is taken, the caller decides if this is a professional, courteous office or an impersonal, impolite one. The decision about whether to do business with this office is an easy one, given that choice. It's just as easy for the assistant to remember to make the best possible presentation of his or her office, agent and services.

Good: "Good afternoon, __________'s office. This is _________; may I help you?"

Bad: "Hello?"

Worse: "Yeah, whadyawant?"

If the agent is unavailable, assure the caller that you will give the agent the message:

> "I'm sorry, but _________ isn't in the office right now. I'll make sure __________ receives your message. Thank you for calling."

Clarity is Everything

In far too many cases, the person who answers a business's telephone mispronounces the company's name, slides over it, mumbles it or speaks so fast the name is lost. Don't assume people know where they're calling. They may be returning a call, and only have your phone number. In any case, speaking clearly not only suggests careful thought, it gives callers the impression that you listen to them as well. Figure 5.4 illustrates some phrases to avoid, and recommended alternatives.

Figure 5.4 Phrases to Avoid

Instead of Saying...	You *Should* Say...	BECAUSE:
"I don't know."	"That's a good question. Let me do some checking and find out for you."	If you don't know, find out: that's your job. Other than sensitive personal or financial information, there isn't anything you can't find out.
"We can't do that."	"Let's see what we can do."	There's no need to tell a caller what you can't do; tell the caller what you *can* and *will* do. Before you give up, give it a try.
"You'll have to..."	"You'll need to..." "Here's what you could do..."	Real estate is a *service industry*: you take orders from the client, not the other way around.
"Hang on a second, I'll be right back."	"It may take two or three minutes for me to get that information. Would you like to hold, or shall I call you back with the answer?"	You won't be "right back," and nothing takes "a second." Don't lie: tell callers *why* they'll be on hold, and for how long.
"No, we didn't get your sign put up today, but we'll get to it tomorrow."	"We weren't able to put up the sign today, but we'll be sure to do it tomorrow."	Never start a sentence with a negative. It conveys total rejection, even if the idea is basically positive.

Level-Elevating Words

Certain words and phrases can defuse an irate caller by elevating the level of the conversation. *Never match the caller's tone of voice*. The caller is free to be nervous, angry, suspicious or delighted; you should always be professional and polite, no matter what. Here are some examples of level-elevating words:

- *"May I . . .?"* Asking permission implies that you recognize the caller's authority. Having given them the authority to say no, they're more likely to say yes.
- *"As you know . . ."* This phrase suggests that you recognize the caller's vast knowledge and experience, and validates their intelligence. They're also unlikely to contradict you, because they'd be suggesting that they *didn't* already know.
- *"I'd like your [advice, opinion] about . . ."* Again, this phrase recognizes that the caller is an authority. People like being authorities.
- *"You are so right."* A more enthusiastic form of "that's right," this phrase includes a friendly pat on the back in addition to a recognition of the caller's impressive wisdom.
- *"Please."* The "magic word" your parents told you about is still magic.

Effective Message-Taking

As a matter of policy, an assistant should try to return all calls within three hours. Remember that what the assistant does reflects directly on the agent; promptly returning phone messages shows that the caller is taken seriously.

The main phone task of the assistant is to make sure that the agent takes only those calls that required his or her personal attention. If the assistant *can* handle it, the assistant *should* handle it.

...FOR EXAMPLE

Caller: This is Alan Agent. May I speak to Bob Broker, please?

Assistant: He's in a conference with a client right now. This is his assistant, _________; may I help you?

Caller: I need to know if 268 Belmont has a two-car garage.

Assistant: I can help you with that. 268 Belmont has a two-car detached garage. Do you have any other questions I can help you with?

Unlicensed assistants should be sure whether state law and office policy permits them to give information about listings over the phone.

Just remember: the real estate assistant is an active member of the agent's team. As an active member, the assistant needs to be able to take on responsibility wherever he or she finds it. If a caller presents a problem, it's the assistant's job to solve it, not pass it along to the agent.

If you must take a message, be sure to get the following information:

- the caller's name, including the correct spelling
- the phone number where the caller can be reached: try to get both a home and work number, and repeat each number back to the caller to check for accuracy
- the message: try to get something specific from the caller

Remember not to push callers too hard. Too much aggressive information-seeking can quickly begin to sound like a police interrogation. Callers often like to remain mysterious. Respect that, but try to get as much information out of them as you can. Never be demanding or rude, however: every call is a current or potential client, and the client is always right.

"Hold, Please"

Hold is probably the most powerful weapon in the telephone arsenal. Like any powerful weapon, it should be used with extreme care. Studies have shown that most callers will hang up after 40 seconds if they're paying for the call. Local callers, or callers to an 800 number, will hold for about three minutes. Even if they don't hang up, however, callers who are left in the limbo of "hold" for more than a few seconds are not getting a very good impression of your agent's services. Being busy is one thing; being rude is another. Further, an angry caller is just going to get angrier the longer he or she is kept on hold, and angry callers never hang up.

As a rule, a caller should never be put on hold until they've been asked permission to do so. After you've asked, be sure to wait for the caller's answer. People will tend to stay on hold longer if they know the name of the person they're waiting to speak to:

> "If you'll please hold, I'll let __________ know you're returning her call."

Signing Off

Few things are more difficult than gracefully and politely getting out of a phone conversation with someone who wants to keep on talking. Here are some suggestions for how to do it.
If you are stuck on the phone with a well-meaning prospect who wants to continue chatting after the business part of the conversation has ended, you might say:

> "Just one more question and I'll let you go . . ."

Of course, you'll need to have a question ready (preferably a yes-or-no type question). However, this sentence serves two useful functions: it signals the conclusion of the conversation clearly yet politely, and at the same time it makes it seem as if *you* are the one taking up the *caller's* time.

Similarly, when you need to return a call from someone you know likes to talk, it might help to begin the conversation by setting limits, saying something like:

> "I just have three quick questions for you:"

If someone asks to put *you* on hold, be cooperative, but set limits:

> "Sure — but please take my phone number in case I need to hang up."

This lets the person know that you are cooperative but busy, and may help shorten the amount of time you spend listening to music.

PHOTOGRAPHY

Assistants are often asked to take pictures of the homes an agent is listing. Pictures are used for advertisements in newspapers, and are often displayed at the real estate office. Even if the assistant is not a trained photographer or lacks an artistic eye, he or she can still take effective photos of properties. Here are a few tips:

- Take several pictures from different angles and distances: the more choices you have, the more likely it is you'll find a good shot.
- It's usually most effective to de-emphasize a home's weakest aspect. Avoid pictures that feature the garage, a cracked driveway, cluttered sideyard or an unattractive neighboring home.
- Pictures usually turn out best when the sun is behind the photographer, fully lighting the subject. However, beware of heavy shadows. Dramatic contrasts of light and shadow are fine in art galleries; they're not effective marketing tools for houses, however.
- Try to emphasize the positive: if a home is very close to one neighbor but has a forest preserve on the other side, take the picture to emphasize the wooded landscape.
- While no one can control the weather, the best home photos are taken on a clear day. Leaves, flowers and grass are nice to see in a listing photo, although rare in the winter. If there's snow, try for a picture that says "wintery charm" rather than "shoveling snow."

SUMMARY

Most assistants begin their careers in the area of office administration. This primarily involves developing and applying organizational systems to the flow of documents and papers within the office, referred to as the paperflow. File organization strategies include alphabetization, separate filing and indexing.

There are two requirements for record-keeping in a real estate office: records must be accurate and current. The information kept in records should be uniform. It is important to keep records of all contacts, transactions and events. A clipping file helps the assistant and agent keep up-to-date on current developments in the industry. A phone directory and the agent's calendar must also be kept current.

Some agents have their assistants perform accounting and bookkeeping functions. These are valuable skills that require special training and, in some cases, licensing.

The telephone is the assistant's most important tool. As the agent's shield against time-demands, the assistant is responsible for screening, prioritizing and following up on calls. If the assistant can handle the caller's question or problem, it should not be passed along to the agent. Phone-flow can be analyzed and controlled. Telephone etiquette and effective telephone techniques are vital to an assistant's efficiency and effectiveness as the agent's first contact with clients and potential clients. Politeness, professionalism, clarity and a positive attitude are important elements. Messages should be taken accurately and completely.

Assistants are sometimes asked to take pictures of homes. There are several considerations in taking a useful marketing photo. These include angle, lighting and emphasizing the positive aspects of the home.

KEY TERMS

activity log
alphabetical organization
buyer packet
change form
clipping files
cross-reference
daily planner
FSBO
index
inventoried
listing packet
office administration
paperflow
pre-listing packet
property disclosure report
purchase agreement documents
shared documents
showing information form

Review Questions

1. Which of the following would *not* be included in a listing papers file?

   a. Purchase agreement documents
   b. Showing information sheets
   c. MLS reporting forms
   d. listing agreement

2. A packet containing marketing information about the agent, maps of the community and information about schools is a

   a. listing packet. c. buyer packet.
   b. pre-listing packet. d. home packet

3. The most important question to ask before creating a file or filing system is:

   a. What is the easiest way to do this?
   b. What do the agent and company want?
   c. What is the quickest way to do this?
   d. What do I want to do?

4. The way a document moves from one person to another in an office is referred to as its:

   a. flowchart c. flowpath
   b. organization d. paperflow

Questions 5, 6 and 7 are based on the following facts:

R, an agent's assistant, was handed a pile of documents. "This is the 123 4th Street sale," said the agent. "Please get it organized." The stack included: (1) a seller's disclosure report; (2) a memo about the buyers (the *F* family), written after their first visit to the office; (3) a showing information form; (4) a letter from the buyer's attorney to the seller's attorney; (5) a listing agreement with the seller (the *W* family); (6) the purchase agreement; (7) the closing documents; and (8) the offer to purchase.

5. Which one of the following lists most accurately show which documents should go in the *W*'s file?

   a. Documents 1, 2, 5, 6 and 7 only
   b. Documents 2, 4 and 8 only
   c. Documents 1, 3, 4, 5, 6, 7 and 8 only
   d. Documents 1, 2, 3, 5, 6, 7 and 8

6. Which documents should go in the *F*'s file?

   a. 2, 4 and 8 only.
   b. 1, 2, 5, 6 and 7 only
   c. 2 and 6 only.
   d. 1, 2, 3, 4, 5, 6, 7 and 8

7. In which file should the lawyer's letter go?

   a. *W*'s only, because it concerns the sale.
   b. *F*'s only, because it's from their lawyer.
   c. Neither *W*'s nor *F*'s.
   d. Both *W*'s and *F*'s.

8. One morning, real estate agent *V* opened the supply cabinet and found the office was out of the yellow legal pads she like to bring to listing presentations. *V*'s assistant had failed to keep:

   a. an inventory. c. the calendar current.
   b. a clipping file. d. expenses down.

9. All phone calls should:

   a. go directly to the agent.
   b. be screened by the assistant.
   c. be answered later.
   d. be screened by an answering service.

10. Acme Exterminators is calling an agent about an inspection problem. If the agent's assistant answers the call, he or she should

    a. take a message that "Acme called."
    b. find out what the problem is, and report it to the agent
    c. ask the agent what to do.
    d. tell Acme, "I don't know what to do!"

Organizing for an Efficient Office

In this chapter, we discuss the practical strategies and systems an assistant can use to help achieve two important goals: efficient work habits and an efficient office. By the end of the chapter, you should be able to apply several different organizing strategies.

You'll learn the importance of using checklists and the four-step method and of planning your day, your year and your career. You will gain some insight into how to determine the most effective way to approach your employer with new ideas. Plus, you will learn several effective hands-on methods of personal organization and time management.

CHECKLISTS

To create an organized, efficient workplace, the assistant must be organized and efficient. A good starting point for establishing a productive environment both for yourself and for your office as a whole is the checklist. A **checklist** is actually a three-step organizing tool:

1. To *create a checklist*, you need to think through a task or situation from beginning to end. To define the goal, you'll need to ask certain specific questions: What needs to be done? What steps need to be taken? In what order should the steps be taken to get it done? By thinking about what you're going to be doing, and by taking a job apart into its individual pieces, you are analyzing the problem, deciding on a solution, and figuring out the best way to achieve your goal.

2. By *following the checklist*, you ensure that each step in the task is completed before you move on to the next step. This helps keep you directed and goal-oriented, and makes you less likely to be distracted.

3. When you're finished, you can *review the checklist*. The completed checklist reminds you of why you undertook this task in the first place. From the finishing point, you can look back over the process you designed and ask yourself if it was the best possible way of doing the job, or if you should try something different next time.

These steps — creation, performance and review — are the fundamental steps to solving any problem in an organized, logical and efficient manner, with or without a checklist.

Another way to remember the system is:

- "Think about what needs to be done . . ."
- "Think about how to do it . . ."
- "Do it . . ."
- "Think about how you did it."

Figure 6.1 illustrates a sample checklist.

While it's healthy for assistants to start out with checklists as they learn new skills within an organization, they should be aware that career growth does not stop there. Many assistants, although well-meaninged, actually create work that doesn't accomplish anything when they sit down and make a checklist for every little thing they do. I'd tell all assistants: when you create and use checklists (which is a good thing to do) *please* be sure to remember priorities.

THE FOUR-STEP SYSTEM

Another way to organize an office into an efficient workplace (and to enhance the real estate assistant's professional image and promotion possibilities as well) is the **four-step business management system**. Becoming a good real estate assistant is a process: it takes time and effort. Many assistants stop short; they feel comfortable waiting for orders from the agent. That is a strategy not only for a dead-end career, but for failure as a professional assistant. The real estate assistant's role is to grow into the agent's business — to move from real estate secretary to licensed assistant to licensed business manager.

There's a saying about assistants that really sums it up: you can always tell a good assistant by what they do when they have nothing to do. If they're not growing, they're going...out the door.

Figure 6.1 Sample Checklist

In the sample below, note how the assistant has broken the day's work down into categories, then checked off each job as it is completed.

Tuesday, October 15

Fieldwork

Set up sign at Benson house and replace stolen sign at Holfield house✔ 10:45
Get lock box for Geribelli house and deliver
Take picture of Swenson house
Take picture of Leopold house
Drop off signs and stuff for Clowen open house with Marcia

Correspondence

Send follow-ups to Burnham open house visitors

Pre Closing

Order title work for Newell sale!!✔ 8:45
Gather CMA stats for Thompson and Richards listing presentations✔ 9:20

Phone

Get hotel info - confirm Jim for NAR conference!!✔ 9:45
Call expired listings from Monday list
Call Sue at Daily News about new display ad

Computer

MLS entries!!✔ 10:30
Work on updating form letters project
Update web page on Internet

Office

Update listing file
Communication meeting at 11
Check inventory in supply cabinet

The four steps to career growth and workplace efficiency are:

1. Organize
2. Anticipate
3. Participate
4. Measure

Organize

The four-step system includes checklists, as already discussed. The checklist is the first phase of business management: the organizational stage. However, it is important to realize that, while checklists are highly effective tools for organizing work, it is not an assistant's goal simply to create them. A checklist is not the means to success; rather, it is a means to get the assistant to the next step in business management.

In this first stage, the assistant should sit down and think about the task at hand, whether it's a filing issue or the question of how to structure a process or arrange office systems. What is that needs to be done? What is the best way to do it? What are the steps involved? Once the problem has been taken apart and thoroughly analyzed, the assistant is ready to get to work.

This first phase should not take up an assistant's whole day. Set aside some time for planning a strategy and constructing a checklist, but make sure it's only the minimum amount of time necessary. An assistant is paid to do, not to think about doing.

Anticipate

One of the first things an assistant needs to do is figure out his or her agent. What does the agent like to do? How does the agent like to see things done? Is there an effective existing procedure? At first, the agent will have to tell the assistant how to do most jobs: what needs to be done and when. If the agent has to tell the assistant when and how to do everything, then the agent is in fact being the assistant. This direct-supervision relationship must be a short one if a long-term assistant-agent relationship is to be established. Usually, the assistant can move into the anticipation phase within three to six months of being hired.

In this phase, the assistant has become familiar enough with the business to actually predict events and anticipate activities so that he or she can take care of issues before the agent even mentions that they need to be handled.

Tools. A team wall calendar that shows the activities of all the members of the agent's team is a useful tool for keeping track of everyone's responsibilities. Similarly, the assistant's day planner will help you anticipate your tasks in advance (refer to Figure 5.2; see Figures 6.2 and 6.3).

Figure 6.2 Daily Priority Planning Checklist

Today's Priorities

Date:__________________

PRIORITY	✓DONE
1	
2	
3	
4	
5	
6	
7	
8	
9	
10	
11	
12	
13	
14	
15	
16	
17	
18	
19	
20	

Figure 6.3 Daily Plan — Short-Term Goal

DO TODAY!

Today's Date:________

Job Description: ______________________________

GOAL:

I want: ______________________________________

No later than: ________________________________

*Because (Benefit)*______________________________

STEPS *(cross off as completed)*:

1.

2.

3.

4.

5.

6.

7.

8.

Participate

As the assistant becomes more and more knowledgeable, skilled and organized (by making effective use of checklists and calendars), he or she will be able to participate more in the business as his or her job description expands. As the day-to-day operations of the office become more second-nature to the assistant, he or she will have to spend less time on paperwork, and will be free to expand in new directions. For instance, the assistant may bring in new innovative marketing ideas, and then implement them, or be completely in charge of the agent's advertising and marketing budget.

Measure

Once the assistant has completely taken over the mundane aspects of the business, and has gone on to become an expert in certain areas, he or she can effectively run the office in the agent's absence. At this point, the licensed assistant will have a full system in place for measuring every activity in the office, such as:

- ❖ Number of calls generated by each listing's advertising, and which publication produced them
- ❖ How much money was spent each year on home brochures, photos and advertising
- ❖ What the yearly marketing budget amounted to and which programs produced the greatest results
- ❖ Which neighborhoods or areas in the agent's region are the hottest, and which have the least activity
- ❖ The reasons why listers chose the agent

Assistants who measure are usually licensed, experienced and work long hours. They also have a strong business relationship with the agent, because they bring knowledge and skills that the agent doesn't have time to gather.

It is important to remember that the assistant cannot grow in business management without the agreement and cooperation of the agent. Further, no organizing systems or structures should be put in place without first telling the agent about them. There may be some unforeseen complication or objection of which the assistant may not have been aware.

Using the Four-Step System

These steps can be implemented on a large scale — that is, they can form the organizing structure for the assistant's career advancement over several years, a process referred to as **macro-organizing**. On the other hand, they can also be used for small-scale project planning, or **micro-organizing**.

On the large scale, the four-step system structures the assistant's professional growth. At first, the assistant spends pretty much 100 percent of his or her time managing the day-to-day work of the office. As the assistant gains confidence and skills, he or she begins to be able to anticipate what needs to be done, and fit it into the organizational framework. Eventually, the assistant becomes a full participant in the real estate business, tracking the performance of the systems and procedures he or she has developed and set in place.

On the small scale, the four-step system works like this: the assistant is given a task. He or she develops an organizing strategy (using checklists) to perform the task as effectively as possible, and tries to anticipate (1) everything that could go wrong; (2) everything that could happen as a result of doing the job; and (3) other jobs that could be done in the same way. The assistant then participates in the system he or she has designed, testing it by using it. Finally, the assistant can measure the success of his or her strategy by determining whether or not it got the job done well. If the assistant wrote a checklist at the beginning of the process, the measuring phase is the time to go back and make sure the checklist has been followed.

PERSONAL ORGANIZING STRATEGIES: TEN TOP TIPS

Often, a new assistant enters a work situation which is less than ideally organized. The agent may have been operating for years on an "as-time-permits" approach to filing, workflow and organization (and, for real estate agents, time rarely permits). Or the agent may have developed work habits and systems that are well-suited for a smaller practice, but not for effective team work. In any case, it's the assistant's job to make sure the agent's business is run smoothly.

So far, we've looked at two good approaches to organization. However, it's important to remember that in order to effectively organize a workplace, the assistant needs to be organized, too. In this section, we'll discuss ten personal organizing strategies: habits and techniques designed to help the assistant ensure that he or she is productive, proficient and business-like in all aspects of his or her professional life. The ten strategies are:

1. Practice Communication
2. Set Goals
3. Hold Regular Meetings
4. Write Progress Reports
5. Prepare a Daily Plan
6. Create a Routine
7. Establish a Learning Base
8. Take Notes
9. Check Your Work
10. Be Professional

Practice Communication

People use the word "communication" all the time, but few people actually do it. Communication is not the same as reporting: communication is a two-way exchange of ideas and information. The most important part of that definition, and the part that is most frequently forgotten, is *two-way*. Good communication involves a communicator and an audience (the person or persons to whom information is being given) in an active relationship. When an assistant communicates with his or her real estate agent, the assistant listens as well as talks. Too often, people "communicate" without listening: that isn't effective communication. An effective communicator is in constant touch with his or her audience, to find out whether they understand the message, whether more information is needed, what they think.

To practice communication means to listen. Listen to yourself (how clearly are you conveying the information?); listen to your audience (is the agent asking questions?); listen to your message (are you answering questions? is the information you're providing valuable?). Always be aware of what you're saying, how you're saying it, and how your audience is reacting to it.

The other end of communication is being a good audience. That is, when someone is telling you something, be an active listener. Really listen to what someone is saying, rather than thinking about what you're going to say next.

How is good communication an organizing strategy? When you think through what you have to say to someone, and when you listen to what others have to say, you avoid having to do things twice.

Set Goals

A good personal organizing strategy is to set goals for yourself. If you always have something to work toward, your work will almost automatically organize itself. You should set **professional goals**: a long-term career plan for yourself. A professional goal could be a promotion or position you want to fill in an office or in the industry. All your other goals, everything you do in your job, should be related somehow to this professional goal. For every task, from sharpening pencils to establishing a marketing plan, ask yourself: how does this fit into my "big picture"? How can I do this job in a way that moves me forward, toward my professional goal?

Long-term goals are job-related, rather than goals for a whole career. That is, an assistant may have a long-term goal of setting up an efficient filing system for the agent. This long-term goal may take many months to accomplish, and will be made up of many smaller tasks. It must also be worked on piece-by-piece, as the assistant's other responsibilities allow. When setting a long-term goal, the assistant should have a clear understanding of how the office or business works and how it could be made to work better. The purpose of any long-term goal is to improve the agent's business and the assistant's workplace. A long-term goal will be made up of numerous short-term goals.

Short-term goals are set for individual jobs. An assistant's career is made up of hundreds of day-to-day short-term goals. You should set short-term goals for everything you do, because setting a short-term goal requires you to think about each task at hand, and to analyze how it should be done.

When setting a short-term goal, you need to ask yourself: how long will it reasonably take me to do this job? When it's finished, what will I have accomplished? How will things have changed or improved as a result of this work? How will doing this job make my work easier or more productive in the future? A good short-term goal will be

- realistic
- appropriate
- constructive

A *realistic* goal means that it can be done, and done in the time allotted. Setting a short-term goal of being a professional basketball player in one week is probably not realistic: it isn't likely to be accomplished at all (for most people) and certainly not in the space of seven days. Setting a short-term goal of improving one's basketball skills in two months is a more realistic goal. Think about what job needs to be done, and how long it is reasonably likely to take.

A goal is *appropriate* if it is related to furthering the agent's business and your career. Going back to the basketball example, the goal of being a professional basketball player is not appropriate for a real estate assistant, because it doesn't further the agent's business or the assistant's real estate career. On the other hand, a short-term goal of organizing the listings file in two months is appropriate and may be realistic (depending on the current state of the listings file).

Finally, a goal is *constructive* if it will help the assistant achieve his or her long-term and professional goals. If the assistant's professional goal is to be the business manager of a real estate office, then improving his or her basketball skills is not constructive. However, organizing the listing files probably *is* constructive.

Every task the assistant performs in a real estate office is **cumulative**. That means that it accumulates, or adds on to past work. Think of each task as a rock you can add to a rock pile of completed tasks. You can stand on the pile to reach upward, toward your professional goal. The higher the pile, the closer you get to achieving your goal. But if your rock pile is going to be a sturdy, reliable platform, you want each component to be of the best quality. Every job you do needs to be done well at the smallest, most basic level.

Many times, your short-term goals will be set for you by the agent. In those cases, you cannot control any of the factors: you just need to do the job in the time required. Some of your long-term goals will also be established by the agent, in your job descriptions. The agent has decided to hire an assistant with certain long-term goals of his or her own in mind. These must take precedence over your personal long-term goals. You should also discuss your professional goals with your real estate agent, in order to find ways to accomplish them.

Figure 6.4 Real Estate Assistant Job Description: Statement of Long-Term Goals

1. To make sure clients are happy and satisfied with our full range of real estate services
2. To put your agent in front of as many buyers and sellers as possible
3. To look for ways to increase income and decrease expenses
4. To handle the administration and coordination of the office so that your agent can focus on prospecting for clients and selling real estate
5. To make sure that you are a profit center by prospecting for clients on a daily basis and by asking for referrals
6. To work hard, to understand your agent's goals and the way he or she thinks, and to try to think like your agent, to anticipate what he or she will need and want
7. To eventually take over all office and business management functions, including but not limited to marketing and financial analysis

---

Figure 6.5 Goal-Planning Worksheet — Long-Term Goals

Statement of Goal:

____

____

____

Start Date: ________________ **Finish Date:** ____________

❖ Ways I can measure my progress toward my goal:

____

____

____

❖ Obstacles:

____

____

❖ What sacrifices will be required?

____

____

❖ What benefits will result?

____

____

Hold Regular Meetings

Real estate offices are busy, hectic places. Frequently, people are so busy that they don't have time to "touch base" with each other. Establishing a schedule of weekly (or monthly) meetings for the team, or for yourself with the agent, is an important step in organizing your work and staying on track.

Because everyone is so busy, the meetings should be held on a regular basis (say, every Tuesday at nine o'clock, or the second Monday of every month). The meetings should be kept short and to the point. That is, there should be an **agenda**: a written list of topics to be covered. The meeting should be informal but not allowed to fall apart into a chat-fest.

If you're meeting alone with your agent, you should write an agenda for yourself: what you want to report and what you want to ask about. Both you and the agent have a lot of work to do, so make sure you use your meeting time efficiently. This is also a good time to practice your communication skills.

For a team meeting, the assistant should structure an agenda so that there is an opportunity for each member to comment, report or raise a question. In either case, the assistant should stick to the agenda and keep things moving. If everyone knows that the meeting will last only one hour, they'll be sure to keep their minds on the business at hand.

An annual retreat *for planning and team-building is an increasingly popular and effective organizing tool: getting people out of the office together in an informal and relaxing location can re-charge professional batteries, create a stronger team bond, and result in new ideas. Retreats can be self-organized or run by a professional trainer.*

Write Progress Reports

Set aside a few minutes each week to write a formal note to yourself about what work you accomplished over the past week, and what you expect to accomplish the next week. Your progress report should have four parts:

1. What I Accomplished
2. Problems and Solutions
3. What Remains To Be Done
4. What I Plan To Do Next Week

In the first part, simply list the jobs you did during the week. In the second part, describe any problems that arose and what you did to solve them: this section may prove valuable later, should similar problems arise again. In the third part, remind yourself about where you are in on-going projects. Finally, set a goal for your next week's work (be sure your goal is a reasonable one).

Prepare a Daily Plan

Preparing a daily plan is similar to setting short-term goals, only in a checklist format. With the agent's direction, you will develop certain tasks that must be performed every day: entering new listings on the MLS, for example, or making a certain number of phone calls to prospective clients. In addition, you can learn from the agent's calendar when certain other jobs will need to be completed — when closing documents need to be distributed, for instance, or when listings need to be renewed. Your own calendar will keep you posted on other deadlines, such as when ads must be submitted to newspapers.

Setting up a daily plan for yourself will help ensure that you get each day's work done. It will also allow you to organize your time so that you can work toward your other goals. (Refer to Figure 6.3.)

Create a Routine

One of the first things an assistant needs to do is establish a routine. Creating and following a routine is *not* the same as getting stuck in a rut. Rather, it means organizing your time in an effective way so that your day is used as constructively as possible. It also helps establish a professional environment and fosters good work habits as well.

The easiest routine to establish involves time. An assistant who is at his or her workplace at the same time every day is showing the agent that he or she is reliable and professional. The agent will know that, if it's 9:00 in the morning, the assistant will be at work. That frees the agent from worrying about who's answering the phones during an early-morning showing or closing. By taking lunch at a regular time, too, and leaving the office at the same time every evening, the assistant establishes a clear and precise section of his or her day when he or she is "on duty." That sort of clear division makes it easier to behave in a professional and organized manner.

Part-time assistants should establish a routine, too. It's best for part-timers to work five days a week, if possible, rather than just "popping in" to work their allotted hours randomly through the week. It's not only better for the office and the agent's business, but it makes it easier for the assistant to develop his or her own professionalism as well.

Establish a Learning Base

An effective, organized assistant uses what he or she learns. That is, every skill and each piece of information you learn should be held on to. Keeping a file of progress reports, meeting notes, daily plans and checklists gives you something to review when new problems arise. You can track your professional growth, too, which is constructive (and encouraging). The real estate assistant's job is one of constant growth and learning, just as the agent's business is constantly changing and evolving. Holding on to past knowledge through a **learning base** is a good way to make sure that change and evolution don't result in disorganization.

Take Notes

Always carry a legal pad and a pen, and always write things down. No matter how good your memory, it's always best to take notes. That way, there's a written record of your instructions, your thoughts and your work. Written notes help you construct your progress reports, remind you of what needs to be done, and provide clear evidence of what you are told to do and when, in case the agent forgets.

Taking notes ensures that your time and the agent's is used efficiently: nothing should ever have to be repeated, and nothing should ever be forgotten.

Check Your Work

This one is obvious: always check and re-check everything you do for accuracy and completeness. There is no room in the real estate business for errors, inaccuracy or sloppy work. Proofreading is a good habit to develop, and numbers should always be checked closely.

Be Professional

Finally, *looking* organized and efficient is an important part of *being* organized and efficient. An assistant who dresses and acts like a professional is more likely to develop good organizational skills and efficient work habits. In short, you are what you look like.

It's also important to *sound* professional, both in person and on the phone. An assistant should develop and use a clear, polite and professional tone whenever he or she is on the job. The assistant represents the company and the agent both inside and outside the office. The assistant is the agent's first key contact with the public, and must present an image that is in keeping with the agent's.

How do you decide what to wear and how to act? Look and ask. When you interview with the agent, look around the office to see what people are wearing. Ask the agent about dress codes and about what kind of public image he or she likes to project. Some agents, for instance, might want to make clients comfortable by presenting themselves as casual, laid-back and informal. In that case, an assistant who showed up every day in a formal business suit might be making a big mistake. On the other hand, an agent who wants to emphasize the real estate business as a financial and legal service similar to law or accounting might not want his or her assistant to wander around the office in jeans and tie-dyed shirts (see Figure 6.6).

GETTING INSIDE THE AGENT'S HEAD

One of the most important keys to achieving an efficient, organized workplace is understanding the agent. It's true: an instinct for basic, common-sense psychology is a very useful skill for a real estate assistant.

I started this business eight years ago and built it up from nothing. Today, I have a list of more than five hundred current and former clients and contacts. Millions of dollars' worth of property passes through my office every year. I am generally considered to be a successful professional, what the magazines call "a savvy entrepreneur." Most people think I'm a pretty smart person with good business sense. I'm good-looking, too (ha ha). But the size of the business got a little out of hand, and so I decide to bring in someone to help out with the paperwork and administrative side so that I can do what I'm best at. So far, so good. But now, suddenly, this new person starts changing things. She starts suggesting new technologies, different filing systems, new marketing strategies. It gets worse: she's actually *good* at it, and I can see a positive difference in how smoothly the office runs. It may not make sense, but I find it a little annoying. I guess it bruises my ego. It's like, I know it was my idea to bring in an assistant, and I know it was a good idea and it's working out OK — more than OK, really. But this business is my baby, and it's like this new person in off the street is telling me that my cute little baby could use some plastic surgery!

And then there's this other thing. I look at this efficient, organized assistant, with all her terrific new ideas, and I can't help but wonder whether I have a dedicated employee or if I'm training the competition. I wonder if she just wants to take over everything.

A real estate business is very much a creature of the agent's personality and vision. When the agent hires an assistant, there may sometimes (certainly not always, but sometimes) be some friction and some reluctance to let the assistant do the job he or she was hired to do.

As an assistant in such a situation, it's up to you to understand the agent's psychology. By determining what the agent really wants, and how best to present what you do, you'll be more effective in the long run. It's important for the assistant to remember, too, that the agent is the boss. If he or she doesn't want a particular system of organization put into place, or if he or she thinks the office runs fine the way it is, then it's the assistant's responsibility to do the best job he or she can within those limitations.

Watch your agent. Watch how he or she interacts with clients, customers and other employees. Does he or she like to chat on an informal level, or are relationships strictly professional? Look at the agent's office. Are there family pictures on the desk? Children's artwork? Photos of pets and friends? Or is the agent all business in the office? How do other employees work? Does the agent like to micro-manage, or is everyone left alone to do their jobs? Are there office lunches and social gatherings, or is the office strictly a place to work? Does the agent have a lot of designations, go to professional seminars and conventions, read trade magazines, business periodicals and management books? Does the agent listen to motivational tapes in the car, or punk rock?

The answers to these questions will tell you a lot about your agent's expectations and personality, and about how you should present yourself and your ideas. A casual agent, interested in new technologies and with a loose management style, might be approached directly with an unconventional idea or new organizing system. On the other hand, a more traditional, conservative agent might be more impressed by a formal presentation that lays out the required expenditures and the resulting savings. You might need to phrase your idea in terms of the high quality of the current system, and how your idea grows from and enhances the way things have always been done.

Here are some other tips for getting along with your real estate agent:

- Know how and when to present ideas: timing is everything. If a closing just collapsed into a shouting match, or if a listing just expired without renewing, it may not be the best time to present your bold new file-reorganization system. On the other hand, depending on the agent, it may be exactly the right time.

Figure 6.6 Sample Dress Code — Sanford Realty Group, Inc.

Dress Standards

Minimum Requirements

Men	Women
Dress shirt	Coordinating blouses/sweaters
Slacks	Professional dress/slacks/skirts
Dress shoes (no sneakers or dockers)	Dress shoes (no flats or sandals)
Socks (conservative)	Hose/nylons/stockings
Ties (tasteful, professional-appearing)	Tasteful jewelry

Unacceptable Attire for Men or Women:

Biker shorts	Leggings	Torn blue jeans
Short/crop tops	Sheer/net tops	Ungroomed appearance
Fluorescent nail polish	Advertisement T-shirts	Unclean/wrinkled clothing

Statement of Appearance Policy

Employees must dress in a manner that is consistent with their responsibilities, with particular attention to the image of our company and interaction with our clients. Employees should address specific questions concerning dress code and appearance policy to their supervisors.

❖ Know your agent: know what he or she likes, know what he or she wants.

❖ Don't take criticism personally, even if it's offered in not-entirely-friendly terms. Develop a thick professional skin, and be prepared to bear the full impact of the agent's bad day.

❖ Be smart, but remember: your boss is a successful professional in an industry where ego is a big factor. Your best bet is to make your boss feel smart.

❖ Ask for more challenges and work, but be sure that you really have room for them; don't try to show off or take over.

❖ It's your responsibility to ask what the deadlines are, and then to meet them. Show the agent he or she can rely on you to get the assigned work done, and he or she will trust you with the extras. Listen, pay attention and follow directions.

❖ Keep your agent informed. Let him or her know what you're working on, what you're thinking about, and what you've accomplished. Don't leave the agent "out of the loop." You expect the agent to treat you like a professional member of a team: you have to treat the agent like a team-member, too.

DEVELOPING PERSONAL SYSTEMS: HANDS-ON TECHNIQUES

So far we've considered a number of more or less big-picture strategies for organizing your work and your workplace. In Figure 6.7, you'll find sixteen additional organizing techniques. While most of them are simply matters of common sense, they don't always seem that way. These techniques have proven highly effective for literally hundreds of successful assistants looking for real-world ways to improve their organizational skills.

Figure 6.8 is another list: the "Ten Commandments" of real estate time-management. Time-management refers to the way an assistant organizes and structures his or her day to make the most effective use of work hours. Again, many of the "commandments" are self-evident. Too often, however, we overlook the common-sense solutions in our search for more fashionable alternatives.

Figure 6.7 Sixteen Top Organizational Strategies for Real Estate Assistants

1. Return all daily phone messages at one time, rather than separately throughout the day.
2. Place all photocopying in a file and do it all at once, rather than going to the photocopier throughout the day.
3. Keep a three-tiered wire basket file on you desk. The top level is Top Priority; the middle level is Do Today; the bottom level is To Do. This will prevent the agent from throwing files all over your desk, and force him or her to prioritize their importance for you.
4. Have one hour of silence during the day. An organized assistant can get an entire day's worth of work done in a single hour of uninterrupted time.
5. Spend the last five minutes of each day writing down the top priorities for tomorrow. Also note questions you'll want to ask the agent in the morning.
6. Before you leave for the day, always make sure your desk is neat.
7. Put all your reading material in a single, handy file. When you are on hold, you can pull out your reading file and do something productive.
8. Record important reminders and organize special projects by using a microcassette recorder. The agent can also use this for letters, reminders and listing information you need.
9. If the agent constantly interrupts your work with questions, try to come to some arrangement that gives you the time you need while still accommodating the agent.
10. Hold short meetings without chairs: if people are standing, they'll want to get to the point and go back to work, rather than lounge around the table swapping gossip and eating donuts.
11. Meet with the agent once a day.
12. Honesty will save you lots of time.
13. Always get right to the point.
14. Pay all bills at the same time, once a month. Keep all bills in one file.
15. Call on the escrows/sale-in-process transactions at the same time every week. Prearrange a time to call loan processors and escrow agents.
16. When someone comes into your office or workspace uninvited, stand up and (politely) walk them toward the door as you answer their question.

Figure 6.8 Ten Commandments of Real Estate Time Management

1. YOU ARE A PROFESSIONAL MEMBER OF A TEAM: UNDERSTAND THAT YOUR TIME IS VALUABLE AND LIMITED.
2. ALL JOBS ARE NOT CREATED EQUAL: SET DAILY AND LONG-TERM PRIORITIES.
3. KNOW WHERE YOU'RE GOING: SET SHORT-TERM GOALS AND LONG-TERMS GOALS.
4. KNOW WHAT YOU NEED TO DO: MAKE A DAILY LIST OF THE THINGS THAT MUST BE DONE.
5. BUDGET YOUR TIME; STICK TO YOUR SCHEDULE.
6. BE FLEXIBLE: BENDING ISN'T THE SAME AS BREAKING.
7. IT'S OK TO SAY NO: IT'S BETTER NOT TO TAKE A JOB THAN TO FAIL TO DO IT.
8. BE ORGANIZED: USE A PLANNING SYSTEM.
9. DON'T BE PERFECT, BE ACCURATE.
10. GET HELP.

SUMMARY

To create an organized, efficient workplace, the assistant must be organized and efficient. There are two important organizing methods: the checklist and the four-step system. A checklist is an organizing tool with three parts: creation, performance and review. The four-step system involves organizing, anticipating, participating and measuring.

The ten personal organizing strategies are: communication, goals, meetings, progress reports, daily planning, routines, learning base, notes, review and professionalism. Every task an assistant performs is a cumulative part of his or her career. It is important to set professional, long-term and short-term goals for yourself.

One of the most important keys to achieving an efficient, organized workplace is understanding your employer. Observation and analysis are vital to success.

KEY TERMS

agenda
checklist
cumulative
four-step business
management system
learning base
long-term goals
macro-organizing
micro-organizing
professional goals
short-term goals

Review Questions

1. A good tool for organizing and charting your progress toward achieving a goal or completing a task is a:

   a. telephone
   b. index
   c. checklist
   d. measurement

2. The four-step system of business management is:

   a. think about what needs to be done; think about how to do it; do it; think about how you did it.
   b. think about how to do it; do it; think about what needed to be done; think about how you did it.
   c. participate; measure; organize; anticipate.
   d. organize; anticipate; participate; measure.

3. Another term for planning projects on a small scale is:

   a. macro-organizing.
   b. anticipation.
   c. micro-organizing.
   d. cumulative-organizing.

4. "Communication" is:

   a. a direct, one-way providing of information, with one person who talks and one person who listens.
   b. a two-way exchange of ideas and information.
   c. an opportunity to plan what you're going to say next.
   d. not part of any organizing strategy.

5. *S*, a real estate assistant, hopes to eventually open his own office. This is a:

   a. long-term goal.
   b. short-term goal.
   c. professional goal.
   d. cumulative goal.

6. A good short-term goal will be:

   a. realistic, appropriate and constructive.
   b. professional, cumulative and realistic.
   c. a career plan.
   d. like a pile of rocks.

7. *T*, an assistant in a small real estate office, decided that monthly meetings would be helpful for everyone. Which of the following should she have for the meeting?

   a. An agenda, a time limit and no chairs.
   b. A checklist and donuts
   c. A daily plan, learning base and long-term goal
   d. A checklist, progress report and daily plan

8. The best way to determine what an office's dress code is:

   a. ask the agent.
   b. trial-and-error.
   c. assume it's informal.
   d. assume it's formal.

9. Look at Figure 6.4. Which goal would be met by requiring the assistant to sit in on a listing presentation as an observer?

   a. 2
   b. 4
   c. 5
   d. 7

10. Look at Figure 6.1. Which category did the assistant think should have priority, regardless of its order in the checklist, and why do you think so?

    a. *Fieldwork*, because it's listed first.
    b. *Pre-Closing*, because all its entries were completed first.
    c. *Computer*, because of the exclamations.
    d. *Fieldwork*, because it has the most entries.

Developing A Marketing Strategy

In this chapter, we'll discuss the importance of marketing a real estate agent's name and services, and examine the fundamentals of marketing theory and practice.

By the end of the chapter, you should be able to identify the qualities of an effective vision statement, describe the processes involved in market analysis, and help an agent construct an effective marketing strategy. You should be able to assist an agent in developing a vision statement and should be able to apply the self-analysis process to your own role as a professional real estate assistant.

REAL ESTATE: A MARKET-DRIVEN INDUSTRY

Real estate is a **market-driven** industry. That simply means that real estate agents provide services to the public that are directly related to the public's demand and desire for particular types and qualities of services. A **provider-driven** industry, on the other hand, would be one that holds a monopoly over a particular product or service that is either a necessity or highly desirable. An electric utility company, for instance, could be considered part of a provider-driven industry. Power companies are not generally subject to intense competition and consumer preferences.

With real estate, however, it's another story. The real estate industry is absolutely dependent on whether or not people want to buy and sell property. The public's decision to buy and sell, in turn, is dependent on a variety of factors over which the real estate industry has little or no control: mortgage interest rates, federal income tax deductions and local property taxes, for example. Other important factors include employment patterns (is a big company moving in or out of an area?); the perceived desirability of a region (is the weather too cold? is the crime rate too high?); and the quality of educational, commercial, cultural and entertainment opportunities. The real estate market depends on which kinds of houses come up for sale, and when they are offered. The list could go on and on, because virtually everything that happens in the nation and the world has some effect on the real estate industry.

The situation is made even more complex by the fact that few people distinguish among real estate agents. As we've observed throughout this book, a real estate agent is an entrepreneur by nature, a small business in practice. Usually, when there are several competing small businesses, consumers make their decisions based on the quality of the product offered. Perhaps the shoes sold by Shoemaker *A* fall apart in a week, but those made by Shoemaker *B* last longer than their wearer's feet. The widespread use of multiple listing services, however, places real estate agents in the position of competitors offering identical products: the Brown house can be shown to potential buyers by not only Agent *A* and Agent *B*, but by pretty much every agent in town. The quality of a real estate agent's product is dependent on the market: who wants to sell their property at any given time.

Faced with more or less identical products, consumers can make their purchase decisions on the basis of price. If one store sells light bulbs for $3 each, and another sells the same light bulbs for $1 each, it's an easy call. Again, however, the situation is complicated for real estate agents. The price of their identical products is also the same, but it is subject to negotiation. An aggressive buyer might be able to purchase a property for less money than a more desperate one. In short, the price of real estate is dependent on the market, too.

So how does a consumer choose a real estate agent? The only factors that distinguish one agent from another is the quality of the service they offer and the image they project. The process of making consumers aware of those factors is called **marketing**. Just as some companies sell products to consumers, the agent's services must be "sold" to the public: people must be convinced that one agent is a more aggressive seller, a more savvy buyer, more honest or more skilled than the others.

Many of the decisions, analyses and techniques discussed in this chapter are things the agent may already have considered. Whether or not the agent has done so, however, the creation of an image and marketing strategy are the agent's prerogative: after all, he or she is the one whose image is being created. However, just as it is important for the professional assistant to have a general understanding of the real estate industry to be effective, it is important to know the basics of real estate marketing theory so that you will both (1) understand why the agent has made the decisions he or she has and (2) be able to start developing new marketing strategies if it becomes your responsibility.

ESTABLISHING A MARKETING STRATEGY

The first step in establishing an effective marketing strategy is deciding what it is you're trying to sell. It's obviously very difficult to convince people to buy something if you don't know anything about what your product does or what makes it better than its competition. The process begins with a vision statement.

Vision Statement: Who Am I?

The answer to the agent's question, "Who am I?" might seem obvious: a real estate agent. But to develop an effective marketing strategy, the answer must go deeper than that. The step after this one involves market analysis: a detailed examination of all the different aspects of the real estate marketplace. Here, the agent needs to undergo a detailed examination of himself or herself, of the business he or she has built, and of his or her values and goals — a more personal kind of **self-analysis**. The result of this analysis will be the agent's **vision statement**: a concise, comprehensive statement of a real estate agent's character and goals.

The objective of this first step is to understand the product — the agent, the business, the services provided, the values and goals involved — so well that it can be defined in just a few sentences. Figure 7.1 shows an example of an agent's vision statement.

Figure 7.1 Vision Statement

Margaret Gerrick ❧ Statement of Purpose

I AM A LICENSED REAL ESTATE PROFESSIONAL, AN ACTIVE MEMBER OF THE NATIONAL ASSOCIATION OF REALTORS® AND A DIRECTOR OF THE NORTHWEST COMMUNITY DEVELOPMENT COUNCIL. MY BUSINESS IS REPRESENTING SELLERS ON THE NORTHWEST SIDE OF THE CITY OF CHICAGO AND NEIGHBORING SUBURBS WHO WANT TO SELL THEIR HOMES QUICKLY AND PROFITABLY, AND ASSISTING THEM IN ALL ASPECTS OF THE TRANSACTION FROM LISTING TO CLOSING AND MOVING. I AM ESPECIALLY EFFECTIVE AT RESOLVING DISPUTES AMONG THE PARTIES AFTER AN OFFER TO PURCHASE HAS BEEN ACCEPTED, AND ENSURING THAT THE SALE CLOSES.

MY CLIENTS ARE CLIENTS FOR LIFE: I OFFER CONTINUING SERVICE AND ATTENTION TO EACH OF MY CLIENTS AND CUSTOMERS, AND ACTIVELY BUILD MY CLIENT BASE THROUGH COMMUNITY INVOLVEMENT AND AN AGGRESSIVE MARKETING STRATEGY. MY GOAL IS TO BE CONSIDERED THE MOST COMPREHENSIVE REAL ESTATE SERVICE PROVIDER IN THE REGION.

There are many ways to self-analyze, ranging from just sitting down in a quiet place for an hour and thinking about the issues involved to filling out questionnaires and looking at past performance records. The most effective method will, of course, depend on what the agent wants. However, no matter what the method, the agent will need answers to the following questions:

- ❖ Why did I go into the real estate business?
- ❖ What is my biggest weakness as a real estate professional?
- ❖ What do I like most about the real estate business?
- ❖ What do I most dislike about the real estate business?
- ❖ What are my most significant professional accomplishments? What is my most significant accomplishment in the last year?

- ❖ Who is my market? What do they want?
- ❖ How much money did I make in the last six months? The last year? The year before that?
- ❖ How many transactions did I have in the last six months? The last year? The year before that?
- ❖ Where do I want to be professionally in one year? In five years? In ten years?

There are many other issues that an agent might want to consider, but these nine questions cover the most significant considerations in developing a vision. The answers to these first questions also set the groundwork for the analysis required in the remaining steps. The questions should be answered in writing.

It is a good idea for an assistant to ask himself or herself these same questions, and to develop a clear, comprehensive idea of his or her own role in the real estate office and marketplace. An assistant's vision statement can form the basis of his or her professional career goals, as discussed in Chapter 6. Throughout this chapter, as we discuss the ways you can help your agent develop his or her vision statement, think about how each issue applies to you as a professional real estate assistant.

Once the agent has undergone a self-analysis, it's time to put all the information (possibly many pages of comments and data) into a comprehensive vision statement. The best way to do that is to read through the answers to the self-analysis and then summarize the most important points. An effective vision statement will include the following:

- ❖ What the agent values about himself or herself;
- ❖ The agent's business focus: where he or she works and what he or she does best;
- ❖ Who the clients are and how they are served; and
- ❖ The agent's professional goals.

Look at the statement in Figure 7.1 again. Let's consider it in pieces, and find out what it says about the agent who developed it.

The first sentence suggests what the agent most values about herself: her real estate license, her membership in NAR and her involvement in a local community organization.

The second sentence is a definition of the agent's business focus, both geographical and practical. It defines where she works and what she does. Note that the emphasis is on the comprehensive nature of her service: "from listing to closing and moving." This agent offers her clients a range of services that is perhaps broader than her competition offers.

Next, the agent has included her major professional strength, which she has decided is her ability to act as a conciliator when troubles arise between sellers and buyers. Her ability to ensure that a sale goes to closing is particularly important to her sellers, who want to get the money and go on with their lives.

In the second part of the statement, the agent states her view of her clients. The expression **client for life** is a common one among real estate agents. It means that their goal is to offer a client continuing service in the future: a seller today is likely to be a seller again in a few years, and today's buyer will be a seller someday. The agent wants to make sure that when the client's next real estate transaction occurs, the agent is there. In this sentence, the agent states her commitment to the client-for-life principle, and explains her strategy for achieving it by offering continuing service and attention.

She also looks to the future by explaining how she plans to grow her business. In this case, she will combine an active marketing program with her community involvement (which she mentioned in the first sentence) in order to expand her client base.

Finally, the agent states her professional goal. Again, as she has made clear throughout her statement, the agent is committed to offering a broad range of real estate services. She wants to be considered a "comprehensive" service provider, so she will have to offer whatever services the market wants or needs. Perhaps this will include offering financial and relocation services in addition to basic real estate sales. Certainly it will require continued professional education.

As you can see, then, a simple statement can include a lot of information about an agent and his or her plans. The vision statement has many different applications, too: in addition to focussing the agent for developing a marketing plan, it can be used as the basis for writing marketing materials.

Gathering information on past sales and creating a questionnaire covering the "vision" issues are two ways in which an assistant can help the agent create a vision statement.

Competitive Analysis: Who Are "They"?

Once an agent has defined who he or she is, it is necessary to define the market in which he or she competes. A **competitive analysis** tells the agent who his or her competitors are and how successfully they compete. This is factual, statistical information: the names of competitors, the number of properties available in the market for specific periods; which competitor sold how many properties. The analysis should include a statement of the **market posture** of each competitor: that is, how do they present themselves to consumers. Determining a competitor's market posture is similar to developing a vision statement for them. The agent needs to consider the competitor's advertisements and marketing materials. Read competitors' brochures and sales letters as if you were a consumer. What do they say about the person who produced them?

Once the agent has defined the competitors, he or she can better analyze where he or she fits in the competitive mix. The agent's sales record should be looked at the same way the competitors' records were considered: how many homes were available, how many did the agent sell? Are there particular neighborhoods or areas in which the agent was stronger or weaker? Are there specific types of property that the agent sells more effectively than others? Among the competitors, which ones handle those types of property? This will identify the agent's main competitors.

Market Analysis: Who Are My Clients and What Do They Want?

Once the agent has defined his or her own identity, and identified his or her competitors, it's time to turn to the market. We already pointed out that real estate is a market-driven industry. The question is, who's driving? The agent will want to know:

- *Who are my clients?* This is strictly factual, **demographic** information such as jobs, salaries, lifestyle, education and family size, as well as information about home values and prices.

- *Where do my clients come from?* There are two ways to read this question, and the agent will want both answers. First, the agent will want to know where the clients come from geographically: are they local people moving locally, or do they come from out of town? If they come from out of town, are they moving long distances (interstate, cross-country or international moves) or short distances (between suburbs, for instance, or from one part of the state to another). The other way to read the question is: how do the clients find the agent? That is, do they come from the agent's telemarketing efforts, newspaper advertisements, open houses, relocation services or word of mouth?

- *What do my clients want?* The information needed to answer this question was gathered during the competitive analysis. The agent will want to know what types of properties his or her clients are looking for. That is, are most of the clients first-time home buyers, or empty-nesters who are selling their large homes in order to move to a condominium in a golf-course community?

The answers to these three questions will help the agent identify the kinds of people to whom he or she must direct his or her marketing efforts. If the market analysis shows that the agent is highly effective with people who are relocating from out of state, or works best with people who are selling and buying starter homes, the agent will have a clearer idea about were and how to "sell" his or her services. For example, an agent who finds that his or her **market niche** — the part of the general real estate market which an agent dominates or seeks to dominate — is first-time home buyers might think about advertising in publications directed at apartment-dwellers. They would be the most likely potential clients.

The process of identifying an agent's market in a useful manner involves two procedures: targeting and segmenting. **Segmenting** means breaking the agent's market up into discreet parts, each with its own special characteristics and requirements. For instance, assume that an agent has 100 past clients. In order to effectively direct his or her marketing efforts, the agent needs to use the market analysis questions to break that group into identifiable pieces: 25 were first-time home buyers; 50 were corporate relocations; 5 were retirees; 20 were moving to bigger houses. Clearly, the largest group of clients are the relocaters, but significant numbers were first- and second-timers. The agent is fortunate to have identified only four segments: there are often many more than that.

Marketing Strategy: What I Want To Do About It

Armed with information about the market, and having segmented it into specific sub-markets, the agent can target his or her marketing efforts more effectively. Targeting was already illustrated in the previous section, where the agent decided to advertise in publications read by apartment-dwellers. **Targeting** means just what its name suggests: using advertising and marketing techniques tailored to appeal to a specific group. Manufacturers do this, for example, when they select certain television shows to sponsor. A car manufacturer will be less likely to advertise during Saturday morning children's programming than during a Sunday afternoon professional football game. The company is targeting the audience most likely to contain drivers. Newspapers and magazines do extensive and detailed research into the demographics of their subscribers in order to attract advertisers. That information is valuable to real estate agents in their marketing efforts as well.

This last step in the marketing process brings us to specific marketing tactics. The agent needs to determine which techniques will be most effective, and how to present his or her services to the various market segments in a way most likely to attract clients. In the following chapters, we'll look at the most prevalent modern marketing techniques: printed materials (including brochures, mass mailings and newsletters) and telemarketing.

The Assistant's Role

For all its obvious importance, the marketing of his or her name and services is frequently a low priority for a real estate agent already swamped with work. Nonetheless, marketing is the key to business growth. Assistants who have marketing capabilities can help expand the business and generate income — a feat that always impresses agents.

Promoting an agent's name in the community is an on-going project, not a one-time or once-a-month task to be checked off a list of daily jobs. It requires planning and persistence, and a considerable amount of time. It is entirely possible that the assistant will have to find time to work on marketing during a day that already seems more than completely filled. However, good marketing is a form of organization; and organization, as we've already said, pays off.

SUMMARY

The real estate industry is market-driven. The main factors that distinguish one service-provider from another are service and image. An agent's services and image are presented to the public through marketing.

A vision statement helps the agent determine the role he or she plays and want to play in the marketplace. The agent must also identify competitors and clients, and decide on the most effective strategies for dealing with each individual segment of his or her market.

KEY TERMS

client for life
competitive analysis
demographic
market posture
market niche
market-driven
marketing
provider-driven
segmenting
self-analysis
targeting
vision statement

Review Questions

1. Real estate is a/an:

   a. market-driven industry.
   b. provider-driven industry.
   c. agent-driven industry.
   d. marketing-driven industry.

2. The major factors that distinguish one real estate agent from another are:

   a. the price and quality of the product.
   b. market posture and price.
   c. the quality of service and image they project.
   d. the quality of service and the price of their product.

3. A concise, comprehensive statement of a real estate agent's character and goals is his or her:

   a. market posture.
   b. vision statement.
   c. market vision.
   d. vision quest.

4. "In 1995, there were 46 houses sold in our region. Of those, Lillian Realty sold 15; Rothschild Real Estate sold 9; Aeronaut 2000 sold 6; Golden Threshold sold 4; and you sold 12."

   This is an example of a:

   a. competitive analysis.
   b. market vision.
   c. demographic analysis.
   d. segmented market.

5. In performing a market analysis, an agent needs to ask: *Who are my clients? Where do my clients come from?* and:

   a. *What do I value about myself?*
   b. *Why did I go into the real estate business?*
   c. *What do my clients want?*
   d. *Who are my competitors?*

6. *Segmenting* refers to the practice of:

   a. using advertising and marketing techniques to appeal to a particular group.
   b. breaking an agent's market up into discreet parts, each with its own characteristics.
   c. selecting a particular part of the real estate market as the agent's niche.
   d. dominating or attempting to dominate a part of the real estate market.

7. *Targeting* refers to the practice of:

   a. using advertising and marketing techniques to appeal to a particular group.
   b. breaking an agent's market up into discreet parts, each with its own characteristics.
   c. selecting a particular part of the real estate market as the agent's niche.
   d. dominating or attempting to dominate a part of the real estate market.

Telemarketing

In this chapter, we will discuss the theory and practice of telemarketing: using the telephone as a marketing tool. We will address the importance of telemarketing in the real estate industry, and present some important skills and strategies for the effective telemarketer.

By the end of the chapter, you should be able to design a telemarketing script and apply good telemarketing practices in a variety of situations.

WHY TELEMARKETING?

The telephone is one of the most important tools of the professional real estate assistant. It is his or her fastest link to the agent's clients and the means by which most customers and clients first contact the agent. Through **telemarketing** — the use of the telephone as an active marketing tool to present an agent's services directly to the public — the agent's message can be brought right past the front doors and directly into the homes of potential clients and customers. Whether that message is as neutral as "I'm a real estate agent and I'm out here if you need me"or as aggressive as trying to convince a FSBO to list his or her house with an agent, the assistant will need a thorough understanding of effective telemarketing skills and techniques. Because, while telemarketing brings the agent's message right into people's homes, it can be a risky undertaking: many people find telemarketing an offensive intrusion into their lives, and will not think kindly of a call "out of the blue." Others mistake telemarketers for therapists, and take the opportunity to tell the caller the story of their lives and troubles. Either way, the telemarketer has failed to use the call to generate new business.

Regardless of its risks, however, telemarketing is a big business. Most people receive several telemarketing calls each week, from charities and cultural institutions looking for donations; insurance companies and construction companies looking for business; from research firms looking for marketing information — almost anyone who provides a product or service is finding some way to look for customers over the phone. Some people are professional telemarketers, who sit in cubicles in vast warehouse-like phone centers, calling people all over the country to market goods and services or to offer or solicit information. For professional real estate assistants, telemarketing is just one of many responsibilities, although some assistants go on to specialize in designing and administering an agent's telemarketing efforts.

In the real estate industry, telemarketing is rarely used to sell specific properties. Like the other techniques covered in Part III, telemarketing is generally a tool to market the agent's services.

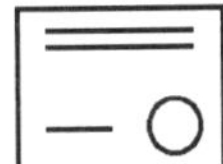

Some state laws may require an assistant to hold a real estate license in order to engage in certain telemarketing activities, such as contacting potential buyers and sellers or soliciting real estate transactions on behalf of the broker or agent.

Cold Calling and Warm Calling

In the telemarketing world, there are two kinds of calls: cold calls and warm calls. A **cold call** is a random call to an individual to convey general information and test market interest. Cold calls are unexpected by the people being called, and are often unwelcome as well. A **warm call**, on the other hand, is a call made with a specific purpose in mind, and which is relevant to a known interest by the recipient in being called.

...FOR EXAMPLE

N sets aside one hour every day to make phone calls to prospective clients by working her way through the local telephone directory. N calls each number in turn and offers to send one of three informational packets (one on home maintenance, one on selling a home, and one on the advantages of buying a home). N is engaged in *cold calling*.

T sets aside one hour every day to call people who have returned a post card that went out in a mass mailing several weeks ago. The postcard said "YES! I'd like more information on the advantages of selling my home with XYZ Realty!" T is engaged in *warm calling*.

Telemarketers and the Law

In order to protect the public from unscrupulous and burdensome telemarketers, the Federal Communications Commission (FCC) has issued certain regulations that restrict and control telemarketing activities. The regulations include:

- If a person who has been cold called asks a telemarketer not to call again in the future, that person's name and phone number must be removed from all lists that the office uses for telemarketing purposes.
- *No home may be called for telemarketing purposes before 8 A.M. or after 9 P.M.*
- Every firm that uses telemarketing techniques must develop and adhere to a written statement on the firm's calling policy, including etiquette, timing, and subject matter.

- ❖ No unsolicited sales materials may be sent through fax machines, computers or telephones.

- ❖ Pre-recorded messages may not be used in calls to any residence unless a business relationship has been established.

In addition to the FCC regulations, many states have additional laws governing telemarketing activities that must be followed.

THE SCRIPT

It fairly often happens in life that we have a conversation with someone and then, several hours later, we remember something important that we should have pointed out, a better choice of words, or a really great comeback. Of course, by the time we think of it we're in the car or eating dinner or taking a shower, so it's too late. Sometimes, these forgotten ideas could have made the difference between success and failure, between making a sale or offending a valued customer.

Politicians, lecturers, educators and trainers — anyone, in fact, who speaks in public on a regular basis — learned long ago the importance of writing down their thoughts and practicing their presentations prior to delivery. Professional communicators, from presidents to salespeople, have all enjoyed success by developing scripts, practicing their delivery, and then comfortably presenting their thoughts to an audience, confident that all their main points will be covered.

Unfortunately, many salespeople have never learned the effectiveness of a script when making sales calls on the phone. They assume that telemarketing is just a matter of asking the right questions under pressure. What usually happens, however, is that they're so busy trying to think of their next questions that they're not listening to what the other person is saying. A **script** is simply the written text of a telemarketing conversation, including alternative statements that permit the telemarketer to respond to a prospect's questions or objections in a controlled, predetermined way. A script relieves telemarketers of the pressure of thinking about what to say next and of keeping the conversation moving. A telemarketer who uses a script can really listen to what the person on the other end is saying, and respond accordingly.

There are other reasons why a script is an important tool for telemarketing:

- ❖ A script provides the telemarketer with a feeling of security, which leads to confidence and an assured tone of voice.

- ❖ Standardization of techniques yields standardized results: this is particularly important when conducting general market surveys or post-closing client-satisfaction polls.

- ❖ A script maintains the telemarketer's focus, and keeps him or her on track.

- ❖ A script helps overcome a natural resistance to calling strangers.

- ❖ Prospects can understand the purpose of the call faster when the telemarketer uses a script, and the telemarketer can convey the information more efficiently. A more efficient call takes up less of the prospect's time, too, which will tend to leave a more positive impression. A long, rambling cold call is not generally a positive introduction.

Developing A Script

The first step in developing a telemarketing script is to determine what you want the call to accomplish. Is the goal to have the agent's name associated with a particular type of service (*"Mark Mullen Puts Your House on TV!"*) or to get the agent in the prospect's living room for a listing presentation? To develop an effective script, you need to know what you want to do, what the last line will be.

After you have decided on a purpose, the next step is to design the flowchart. A **flowchart** is a graphic, step-by-step illustration of a process (in this case, a telephone conversation). The flowchart lets you anticipate the prospect's responses to your questions, so that you can make the script fit as many contingencies as possible. The flowchart is the skeleton of your telemarketing strategy; your script is the skin that covers it. Figure 8.1 shows you a simple telemarketing flowchart.

Once you have drawn the plan of your conversation in the form of a flowchart, you can fill it in with your script. Remember to move backward from your ultimate goal, so that each positive response (a "Yes" box in the flowchart) moves your conversation toward that goal.

Include **open-ended questions** (questions that can't be answered with a simple yes or no, such as "How long have you owned your home?" or "What would you like best in a new home?"). Open-ended question force the prospect to become involved in the conversation.

In writing a script, the assistant needs to strike a careful balance between being too pushy and not being pushy enough. You will need to offer as many positive benefits to the prospect as you can, but beware of being so enthusiastic that the prospect feels like he or she is being overwhelmed. Ask frequent questions, but be sure to steer away from questions that could end the conversation before you're ready. Most people think visually; using descriptive words helps prospects understand what you're talking about.

You should use simple, clear language without sounding too informal or using slang. Remember that this is a conversation, not a speech: provide plenty of opportunities for questions, even if only to reinforce what you just finished saying.

Once you've written a complete script (including "answers" from your prospect), reduce it to a topic outline. Then, by reading through your outline several times, turn it into a conversation. Prospects are rarely impressed by being cold called and then read to over the phone. Make sure your presentation flows like a conversation. Tape recording yourself, practicing in front of a mirror, or actually working through practice calls with friends and family members will help keep you from sounding like you're reading. Remember: never practice on a prospect.

Figures 8.2 and 8.3 are tools to help you organize your script. Figure 8.4 is a sample script.

Figure 8.1 Telemarketing Flowchart

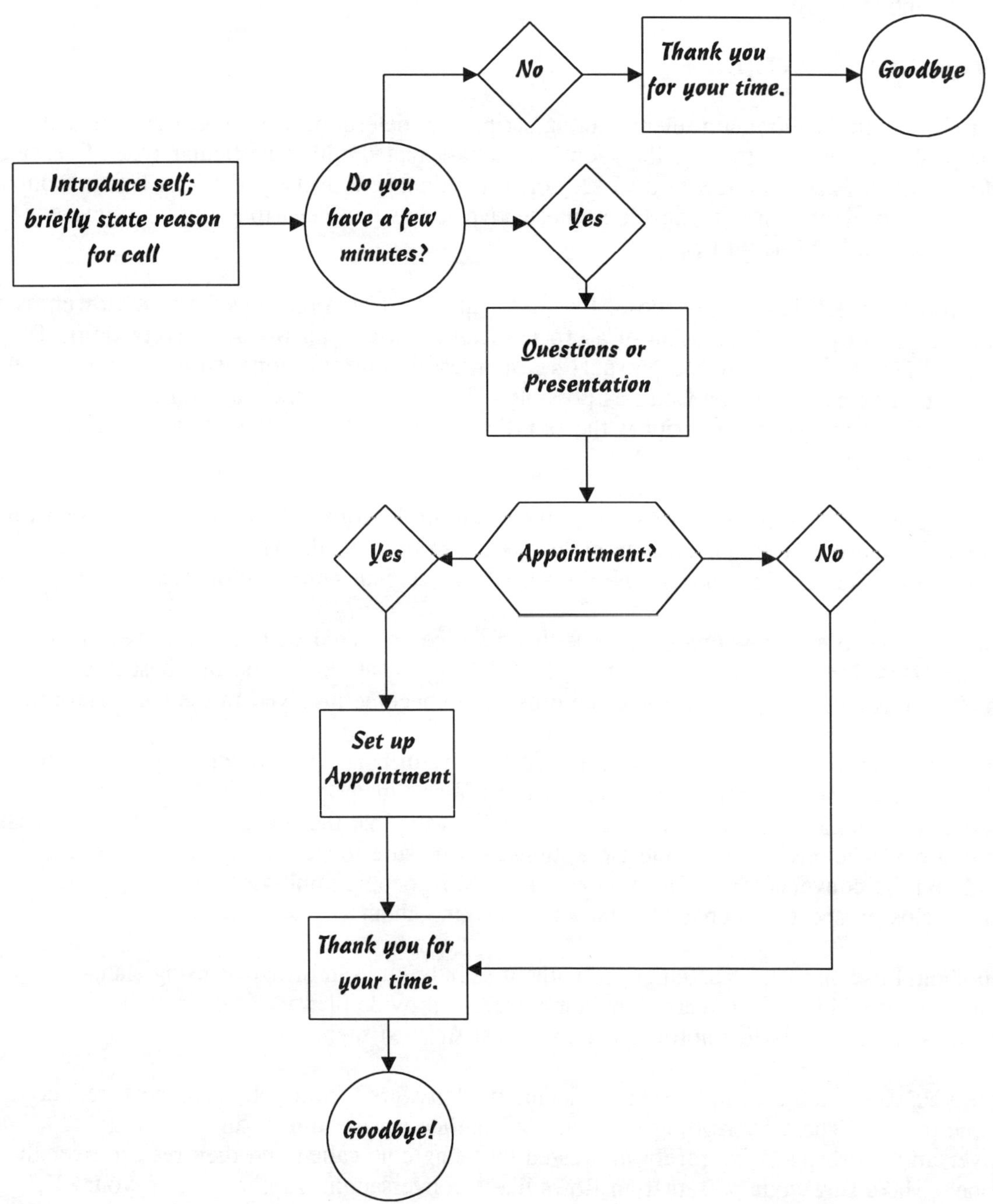

Figure 8.2 Target Script Organizer

This form will help you plan your script by identifying the key features of the call.

✔**Describe the major goal of this script (the reason for the call):**

____

____

____

✔**List and describe any additional objectives:**

____

____

____

✔**Describe the agent and service being offered:**

____

____

____

✔**Describe the type(s) of prospect(s) being contacted (age, sex, location, etc.):**

____

____

____

✔**List the major benefits of working with the agent or company:**

____

____

____

✔**Why should the prospect act now?**

____

____

____

Figure 8.3 Responses to Anticipated Objections

The following form is designed to help you plan your responses to a prospect's possible objections.

"I'm sorry, I'm not interested."

"I'm sorry, I can't do anything unless I talk to my [husband/wife/lawyer] first."

"I don't need a real estate agent; I can sell my own house."

"I don't have time for this right now."

"I'm sorry, but I've had really bad experiences with real estate agents."

Figure 8.4 Sample Telemarketing Script: FSBO Survey

Hi, my name is ______________. I work for ______________ [agent], the leading real estate broker in ______________ [city]. I know you're selling your home yourself, and we respect that. ______________ [agent] has asked me to conduct a quick survey of all the people who are selling their own homes, like you, in our area, to find out why they made that decision. May I take a minute or two of your time to ask you a few questions?

NO: That's fine. You know, ______________ [agent] has put together a package designed to help people like you who are selling their own properties. Could I send you some information about that?

> YES: Great! I'll get that out to you in the mail this afternoon. *[make a note to follow up in three days]*
>
> NO: OK. Let me ask you this before we hang up: which of your friends, family or co-workers might need our help selling their homes? [LIST] Great! Thanks for your time,

YES: Great!

1. Why did you decide to sell?
2. Where will you be moving?
3. How soon do you have to be there?
4. How long have you owned your home?
5. How did you decide on an asking price?
6. What methods are you using to market your property?
7. Are you prepared to negotiate your price with a buyer?
8. Why did you decide to sell yourself?
9. If you listed with a broker, what services would you expect?
10. What, to you, is the most important thing about moving?

Thanks for your answers. They were very helpful. May I arrange an appointment for you to meet with ______________ [agent] to discuss [his/her] ideas about how you can get the most for your home?

YES: Great! Would 7 or 8 tonight be more convenient?

NO: That's fine. ______________ [agent] has put together a package designed to help people like you who are selling their own properties. Could I send you one?

> YES: Great! I'll get that out to you in the mail today. *[make a note to follow up]*
>
> NO: Let me ask you this before we hang up: do any of your friends, family or co-workers might need our help selling their homes? [LIST] Great! Thanks for your time!

Telemarketing Etiquette

The following are some tips for successful and effective telemarketing activity.

- ❖ ***Avoid uncertain and negative language.*** The words you use should make you sound absolutely certain, confident and positive about your topic. Words like *if*, *maybe*, *possibly*, *hope*, *try*, and *sometimes* should be avoided. Similarly, negatives like *can't*, *won't*, *don't*, and *no* should not be used. Your choice of words sends an instant message about you, your agent and the services being offered. Use positive language (*beautiful*, *luxurious*), dynamic words (*energetic*, *leading edge*, *powerful*) and inclusive pronouns (*we*, *us* and *our* instead of *you*, *me* and *I*).

- ❖ ***Never use a monotone.*** As you work through your telemarketing script, you should try to sound like you're awake and alive. You should try to sound alert but relaxed: don't speak too quickly or too loudly. Pronounce words clearly.

- ❖ ***Be interested in the person you're calling.*** Remember: you've invited yourself into someone's house. The least you can do is to be interested in what they have to say. If prospects feel that you're calling *them* personally, rather than just working your way through a list, they're more likely to stay on the line and listen to what you have to say. If you sound interested and committed to your topic, the prospect is more likely to pay attention, too. Keep in mind that you were the farthest thing from your prospect's mind just a few seconds ago, and their inclination is probably to just hang up and get back to whatever they were doing before you literally interrupted them. Be polite, be interested and be interesting.

- ❖ ***Control your environment.*** Where you are when you call is important in telemarketing. You should select a quiet place with no distractions. You should have a comfortable chair, good lighting, and nothing on your desk to play with while you talk. No interruptions should be permitted. If you use a **headset** (a telephone receiver equipped with headphones and a small microphone), you can be free to stand, walk around, and use your hands and arms when you speak — just like you would in any conversation. A speaker phone is not a good idea for telemarketing: despite advances in technology, you may sound like you're talking from the bottom of a well.

- ❖ ***Use a good "telephone voice."*** A good telephone voice sounds alert. Its tone is varied and expressive, and always conversational. Speak clearly, and enunciate. There is a tendency to slur middle syllables or drop consonants off the ends of words: don't do that. Remember that you are a human being talking to another human being. Be careful not to talk *at* the caller, but communicate through your voice that you are interested in what he or she has to say, and have his or her best interests at heart.

- ❖ ***<u>Never</u> be rude.*** If a prospect becomes angry, rude or insulting, don't respond. Unpleasant as it may be, it's the prospect's right to be as nasty as they want: they didn't ask you to call, and you've interrupted their lives. *There is <u>never</u> any excuse for a telemarketer to respond to a prospect's angry, rude or insulting behavior by being angry, rude or insulting.* If a call gets out of control, you can always terminate it politely by saying something like, "I'm afraid I've called at a bad time. I'm so sorry to have bothered you." Be sure to make a note of the incident.

Following these basic tips will help you pass the **5-second hurdle**: the first five seconds of a telemarketing call when the prospect is most likely to say "Sorry, not interested!" and hang up before you finish introducing yourself. Once you've passed that hurdle, the prospect has essentially said, "OK, I might be interested: give it your best shot." Remember as you design your script that the prospect is in control, and can end the conversation at any time.

Finally, don't feel bad when people hang up on you — and people *will* hang up on you. Just remember that hanging up is just a prospect's short-hand way of saying "No, thank you." It isn't personal. They don't know *you,* they're not angry with *you* (even if they say something unpleasant before they hang up), they're not being rude: *they're just hanging up the phone.* Make a note on your call sheet that they are uninterested, and go on to the next prospect.

SUMMARY

The telephone is the assistant's most important tool. Telemarketing is the use of the telephone as an active marketing tool to present an agent's services directly to the public. Certain telemarketing activities may require a real estate license. Telemarketing is regulated by the Federal Communications Commission. There are two kinds of calls: cold and warm.

A script is an essential part of a telemarketer's job: it provides a feeling of security, provides standardized results and ensures focus. In developing a script, the assistant/telemarketer needs to think about what the call is intended to accomplish. Various responses should be anticipated. Telemarketing is most effective and successful when telemarketing etiquette is observed.

KEY TERMS

cold call
five-second hurdle
flowchart
headset
open-ended questions
script
telemarketing
warm call

Review Questions

1. "Telemarketing" refers to

   a. Marketing an agent's services through the active use of television commercials.
   b. The active use of the telephone to market specific properties for sale.
   c. The active use of the telephone to market an agent's services directly to the public.
   d. The use of the telephone as a tool for making offers on listed properties.

2. "Hello, my name is *L*, and I work for BNM Realty Services. May I take a few minutes of your time to explain the advantages BNM offers to people who want to sell their homes?" This is an example of the

   a. beginning of a cold call.
   b. beginning of a warm call.
   c. proper use of a monotone.
   d. use of positive words.

3. "Hello, my name is *L*. I just wanted to follow up on the information package you asked us to send out last week. Did it answer your questions, or is there something I can help you with?" This is an example of the a/an

   a. cold call.
   b. warm call.
   c. improper use of a monotone.
   d. use of positive words.

4. Which of the following would *not* violate the FCC's telemarketing regulations?

   a. Making a cold call at 7:45 A.M.
   b. Sending out a mass mailing by fax.
   c. Leaving a person's name on the "call list" after they've asked not to be bothered.
   d. Making a cold call at 7:45 P.M.

5. All of the following are advantages of using a script in a telemarketing call, *except*

   a. a feeling of security and confidence.
   b. the squares, circles and arrows keep things organized.
   c. it helps the telemarketer stay focused.
   d. prospects can understand the purpose of the call faster.

6. A graphic, step-by-step illustration of a telephone conversation is referred to as a

   a. script
   b. checklist.
   c. flowchart.
   d. call plan.

7. "What kinds of services would you expect from a full-service real estate agent?"

   This is an example of a/an

   a. scripted flowchart question.
   b. open-ended question.
   c. yes-or-no question.
   d. prospect answer.

8. "So, I thought that maybe, if you weren't uninterested, I might be able to set up a possible appointment, if you want."

   Is this a good telemarketing sentence?

   a. Yes, because it is informal in tone.
   b. Yes, because it is not too pushy.
   c. No, because it uses too many words that suggest uncertainty.
   d. No, because it fails to use inclusive pronouns.

Newsletters, Brochures & Direct Mail

In this chapter, will discuss the importance of printed advertising materials to an agent's marketing effort. We will examine the elements that make up an effective brochure, newsletter and direct mailing.

By the end of the chapter, you should be able to recognize the basic elements of graphic design and understand the appropriate use of the various types of printed marketing materials.

ADVERTISING: MAKING MENTAL CONNECTIONS

The purpose of advertising, like the purpose of telemarketing and the purpose of an agent's marketing efforts in general, is to get the agent's name into the marketplace. If people make a mental connection between the agent's name and the idea of a real estate transaction, they're more likely to call the agent when the time comes to buy or sell property. It's even better if the mental connection the public makes also includes associations with ideas like *competence*, *trustworthiness*, *professional*, *successful* and *efficient*. Advertising makes and reinforces in the public's mind the agent's presence in the industry and effectiveness at what he or she does.

This chapter focuses on the three main types of print advertising: newsletters, brochures and direct mail. While there are others — display ads, business cards, and billboards, for example — these three are the most commonly used. They are also the three forms of advertising that assistants are most frequently called upon to work with. A basic understanding of the design, purpose and effectiveness of each of them will help the assistant prepare a strong and productive marketing strategy.

BROCHURES

A **brochure** is a printed booklet, pamphlet or even a single-page letter that provides simple, basic information about an agent or office in an eye-catching, attractive and readable way. It's important to remember, when designing an informational brochure, that it is not intended to be an in-depth analysis of the agent's background and services, or a full-scale listing presentation. Rather, a brochure should be brief. The emphasis should be on its **visual interest**: the way it attracts attention to itself and "lures" people into both taking it *and* reading it.

Designing An Effective Brochure

Professional graphic designers spend years of education and training to learn the most effective ways to design printed materials. A real estate assistant is not expected to be a graphic designer; however, he or she should be aware of the fundamentals of designing printed products in order to create quality materials: a real estate agent's brochures do not have to be professionally designed to be effective.

Just as in planning any marketing strategy, it is important to first identify the purpose of the brochure. The assistant should ask the following questions:

- ❖ *Why does the agent want a brochure, rather than (or in addition to) another form of printed advertising, such as a newsletter or direct-mail campaign?* There should be a good reason to produce a brochure, particularly because a full-color, multifold or multipage glossy brochure can be expensive to print.

- ❖ *Who will be receiving the brochure?* The content and appearance of the brochure should be targeted to the appropriate market. Having already done a thorough market analysis, the assistant may be able to answer this question easily. However, you may need to make adjustments. For instance, if only one brochure is going to be produced and then used as a general introduction, it must be suitable for any type of client the agent is likely to have.

- ❖ *Where is the brochure going to be circulated?* This question is directly related to the previous one. Will the brochures just be stacked on the receptionists desk or handed out on the street corner? Either way, they will be available to a large, random and very diverse audience. Will the brochure be sent out in a mailing? In that case, you know that it should address the expectations and needs of people on your mailing lists. Will it be given to potential listers before or during a presentation? Then it should emphasize their interests.

- ❖ *What will it look like?* Will it be a booklet with several pages, a **bi-fold** or **tri-fold** format? (see Figure 9.1) Will it be on glossy paper for a slick, professional look, or on a heavy, textured paper to look more like a formal invitation? Will it have photographs? What **typeface** or **font** (the style of the letters) will be used? (see Figure 9.2)

Figure 9.1 Bi-Fold and Tri-Fold Formats

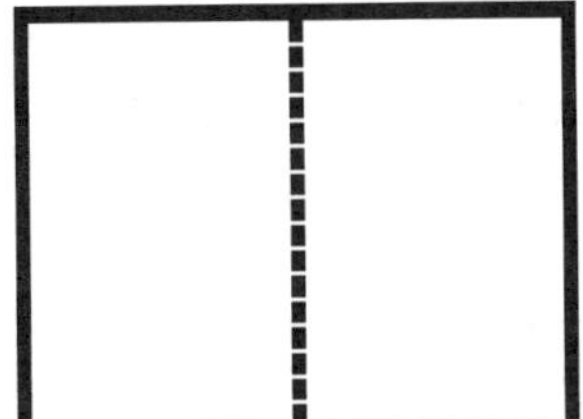

Bi-Fold *— 8½ x 11-inch sheet of paper folded into a four-page, 8½ x 5½-inch brochure; or 8½ x 22-inch paper folded into a four-page 8½ x 11-inch newsletter.*

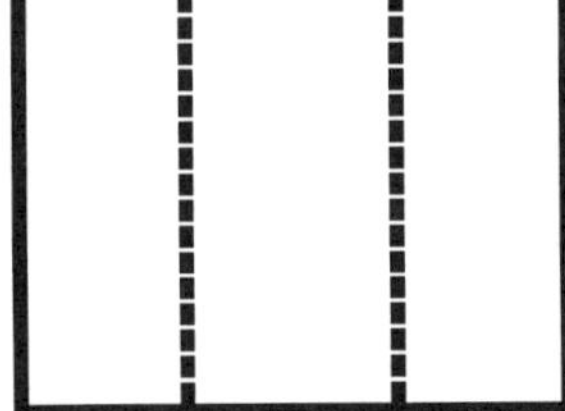

Tri-Fold *— An 8½ x 11-inch sheet of paper folded twice into a six-panel brochure. Each panel measures 8½ x 3⅔ inches, or, if 8½ x 22-inch paper is used, each panel measures 8½ x 7⅓-inches.*

Figure 9.2 Typefaces

All the different typefaces, or fonts, illustrated below are used in various parts of this book.

Rr Rr Rr Rr

RR R Rr Rr Rr

- *How much information should be in the brochure?* Again, this question is related to the others. The amount and type of information provided will depend on what the brochure's purpose is; who its potential audience is; and the brochure's design (lots of pictures or white space may mean fewer words). All these factors determine the style and content of the brochure.

Photograph

A photograph of the agent is an important part of a brochure's effectiveness. It lets people associate a face with the name and all the good things the brochure tells them about. The photograph should be taken by a professional photographer.

The photograph should be a recognizable likeness of the agent's everyday appearance. The agent has probably found his or her own style of professional dress, appearance and behavior. A successful agent's style depends, like everything else, on the demands and expectations of the market. In a conservative, upscale community, an agent is likely to adopt a different style than one who works in a casual college town. A "big-city" agent's style would probably be out of place in an agricultural community. The point is, the brochure photo must look like the agent, or the whole point of associating a face with the name is lost. Time and money has been wasted if the person who shows up on the potential client's doorstep to make a listing presentation is not the same person whom the homeowner saw in the brochure. Be certain that the photographer understands the importance of the agent looking "real."

Design

Good graphic design is an important part of a brochure. You can get ideas by looking at past brochures, and those used by other agents in the office as well as those used by the competition. Books are available in bookstores and the library that will show you the basic principles of modern graphic design. In general, however, the following guidelines should be used:

- Use *color* if you can. Color is eye-catching and interesting. Try to select colors that are bright, but not lurid or clashing (remember, you're selling a real estate agent, not a rock star).

- Use *creative graphic elements*. Bullet-point lists (such as the one you're reading now) are a highly effective brochure device, because they break up a big block of text into manageable units, and focus the reader's attention where you want it to be. You can use dots as bullets, or little houses or "for sale" signs if you feel creative. Putting borders or frames around pictures or text, or highlighting important text with blocks of color are effective methods, too.

- Use *headlines*. When people read newspapers, they skim the headlines for interesting stories, and then read the ones with attention-grabbing headlines. Use headlines in your brochure, too: "***Thirty Years of Success!***" or "***I Will Sell Your House in 60 Days — Guaranteed!***" would be more likely to attract attention than "***I'm a Real Estate Agent.***"

- Keep the content *short and snappy*. A marketing brochure is not a novel. Highlight the agent's education and real estate background; his or her years of success; and the comprehensive services offered. If the agent is active in community service, that may be a relevant fact. Similarly, if the agent has professional designations, they might be included to show his or her interest in continuing education. Quotes from satisfied former clients are effective, as are quotes from the agent. If the agent has created a vision statement as part of his or her marketing effort (see Chapter 6), that may also be a useful place to look for effective brochure content. Of course, the content of your brochure will depend on the market you've targeted.

NEWSLETTERS

A newsletter is an effective advertising tool, because unlike a brochure it does not present itself, at least directly, as an advertisement. Rather, a **newsletter** is a tool for providing information that its readers find interesting or relevant to their real estate needs. But all the time that the newsletter is providing helpful information, it is also saying "This helpful information is being provided for free by a real estate agent who really cares about keeping me up to date on the most recent developments that may affect my finances and lifestyle." Now *that* is not a bad message to send into people's homes. Studies have suggested that newsletters sent to former clients double the likelihood of repeat business and dramatically increase the number of referrals.

Format

Like a brochure, a newsletter can come in many different formats. Some newsletters are only one page long (also called **fliers**), while others are in a bi-fold format. Longer newsletters can be six pages (a bi-fold with a single center page) or eight pages (two bi-folds together). Newsletters can have headlines and text only, or include drawings and photographs, depending on the production technology available.

Newsletters should generally be on high-quality paper, so they feel substantial in the reader's hands. Black ink on colored paper is an attention-getting device that can be achieved with minimum expense.

Newsletters (as well as brochures and other printed marketing materials) used to be expensive and complicated to produce. Today, however, relatively inexpensive computer software is available to help design, produce and print attractive newsletters. With a little practice, an assistant should be able to put together a professional-looking newsletter in a reasonable amount of time. Software for generating newsletters and brochures is available in computer supply stores as well as through advertisements in real estate publications.

Content and Design

The same design and content issues that are important for brochures apply to newsletters as well (see discussion above). Articles should be short and to the point, written in a clear and informal style, but professional, not chatty.

A newsletter should contain a mix of news and marketing related articles. A newsletter's "news" articles might include such topics as:

- ❖ interest rate changes
- ❖ new real estate laws that affect homeowners, such as disclosure requirements, changes in property tax laws and zoning issues
- ❖ helpful home maintenance advice, or techniques for choosing a moving company or home decorator.

On the other hand, the newsletter's "marketing" articles would include:

- ❖ sales statistics for the agent or office
- ❖ introductions of new team members
- ❖ stories about homes just listed, just sold or with price reductions.

Distribution

The newsletter should be distributed in a number of ways. It should obviously be mailed to current and former clients (as part of the agent's "client for life" commitment). The newsletter could also be mailed to FSBOs (many of whom will eventually list with an agent); other agents in the company; cooperating agents; and the agent's list of prospects (the "farm" discussed below). Other potentially profitable recipients include contacts in the lending, legal, home inspection and appraisal industries.

Newsletters should be included in listing and buyer packets, and should be handed out to walk-ins and mailed to people who call about specific listings.

DIRECT MAIL

Direct mail is one of the most expensive marketing options available, although it can also be one of the most effective. It is different from a **mass mailing**, which refers to the practice of sending identical letters or brochures to multiple recipients in a targeted market. Essentially, **direct mail** is the marketing strategy of preparing *individualized* printed materials and mailing them to *specific* people in a targeted market. Those people's names and addresses may be obtained by purchasing a mailing list from a commercial provider (in which case the agent may specify the target demographics and receive a list of people in his or her region who fit those criteria) or they may come from the agent's own "farm." A **farm** is a real estate term that refers to the business region served by the agent, which the agent considers his or her "own." The people in that region are like plants to be cultivated and cared for until they're ready for harvest — that is, until they're ready to buy or sell property with the agent's assistance. The care and cultivation includes telemarketing efforts, newsletters and direct mailings.

It's a good idea for an assistant to develop his or her own "farm," too. This demonstrates dedication and initiative, and helps the assistant build a base of contacts and resources that may be helpful in the future. Likely places to start include social, recreational and athletic clubs, charitable or religious organizations or other community groups to which you may belong. You might also consider sending out postcards announcing that you are now affiliated with the agent.

Creating a Direct Mail Letter

The direct mail letter is not as complicated to produce as newsletters or brochures. In essence, the direct mail letter is simply a standard marketing letter with blanks left to be filled in. The letter should be printed on the agent's letterhead, and **personalized** with the recipient's name both in the salutation and in the body of the letter. Making a letter seem more personal is key to gaining the reader's trust.

Personalizing can be accomplished with amazing efficiency with the help of computers and word processing software. For instance, WordPerfect® 5.2 includes a **mail-merge** function that allows information from multiple documents to be combined into one. Mail-merge can be used to produce personalized letters as well as mailing labels or printed envelopes. In WordPerfect®'s mail merge, for example, there are three files:

1. the **primary file**: the form letter itself, with the places to insert personalized information indicated as numbered [FIELD]s;

2. the **secondary file:** the list of personalized information, in the same order as it will appear in the letter; and

3. the **merged file:** the document in which the primary file's form letter and the secondary file's information have been combined into a single, personalized letter suitable for direct mailing.

The information to be inserted in the form letter may be displayed as either a table or list. Each insertion item is referred to, in WordPerfect®, as a **field**. For an example of how this works, see Figure 9.3.

While the processes for merging files may differ from program to program, the fundamental principles are the same: two files are combined into one, creating the illusion of a personal letter from one individual (the agent) to another (the prospect).

Writing a Direct-Mail Letter

The letter's tone should be informal and informative but not chatty. The letter should get to the point quickly, and close. Figures 9.4 and 9.5 at the end of this chapter illustrate sample direct mailings.

Figure 9.3 Merging Files

Files to be merged may be in either a list or table format. Both formats are illustrated here. See Figure 9.4 for a sample merged letter generated from these files.

I. FILE DATA IN LIST FORMAT: *each line is a field*

Dr. Margaret PhillipsENDFIELD
210 Regency DriveENDFIELD
New Wabash, West Carolina ENDFIELD 01010ENDFIELD
Dr. Phillips:ENDFIELD
the relocation of the CyberDex plant to New WabashENDFIELD
Dr. PhillipsENDFIELD
ENDRECORD
Mr. and Mrs. Rodney PrendennenENDFIELD
4568 West South StreetENDFIELD
Raven Acres, West Carolina ENDFIELD 01011 ENDFIELD
Mr. and Mrs. PrendennenENDFIELD
the new intercity commuter trainENDFIELD
Mr. and Mrs. PrendennenENDFIELD
ENDRECORD
Stanley R. WaschowitzENDFIELD
39 Parnell WayENDFIELD
Loverly, West Carolina 01032ENDFIELD
Mr. WaschowitzENDFIELD
the relocation of 285 CyberDex employees to our areaENDFIELD
Mr. WaschowitzENDFIELD

II. FILE DATA IN TABLE FORMAT: *each cell is a field*

FIELD: FULL NAME	*FIELD: ADDRESS*	*FIELD: CITY/STATE*	*FIELD: ZIP*	*FIELD: NAME*	*FIELD: REASON*
Dr.Margaret Phillips	210 Regency Drive	New Wabash, West Carolina	01010	Dr. Phillips	the relocation of the CyberDex plant to New Wabash
Mr. and Mrs. Rodney Prendennen	4568 West South Street	Raven Acres, West Carolina	01011	Mr. and Mrs. Prendennen	the new intercity commuter train
Mr. Stanley R. Waschowitz	39 Parnell Way	Loverly, West Carolina	01032	Mr. Waschowitz	the relocation of 285 CyberDex employees to our area

When composing a letter for a direct mail campaign, the assistant should not expect the reader to spend a lot of time reading it. The answers to the following questions will help you compose a more effective direct mail letter:

- *Who will be getting this letter?* What does your target audience expect from a full-service real estate agent? If you know your audience, you'll have a better idea of what to write and how to write it. Imagine your target market as a single individual, and write a letter to him or her just as you would to any other person.

- *What is my point?* Write down the basic idea you want to convey in a single sentence. While you probably won't use this sentence in your direct mail letter, it will help you focus on your main issue. In the letter illustrated in Figure 9.4, for example, the main idea might be expressed as "Now is a good time to sell, and Alicia is the person to do it."

- *How would I convince myself?* Think of four or five really convincing examples or arguments that support your one-sentence main idea. Then pick the best two to use in your letter.

A piece of direct mail is usually received with about as much enthusiasm as a telemarketing cold call. No one is really fooled by electronically personalized mail, and direct mail letters are often viewed as "junk mail" and thrown out before they're opened. One way around this problem is to make the letters look as really personal as possible. Hand-address the envelopes (so they don't look mass-produced), and make sure the agent's signature is hand-written, rather than stamped.

Figure 9.4 Direct Mail Letter — Merged

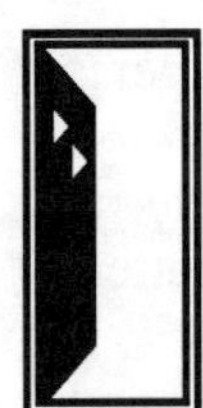

Golden Threshold Realty, Inc.

1515 Marigold Centre Drive, Centerton, West Carolina 01012

From the Desk of *Alicia Agent*, REALTOR®

September 25, 1996

Dr. Margaret Phillips
210 Regency Drive
New Wabash, West Carolina 01010

Dear Dr. Phillips:

There has rarely been a better time to sell your house than right now. Low interest rates and the relocation of the CyberDex plant to New Wabash have made local homes such as yours increase dramatically in value!

Dr. Phillips, I have been fortunate to serve many happy clients, and I would very much like to put my twenty years of success to work for you. When the time comes that you need a competent, professional real estate adviser, please remember Alicia Agent of Golden Threshold Realty. Or, if you know of someone who is thinking of purchasing or selling real estate, please give them my card. I've enclosed a card for you to give away, and a refrigerator magnet for you to use.

I've also enclosed a postcard that I would encourage you to return. If you do, I or my assistant, Pip Havisham, will give you a call to answer any questions you may have, or to set up an appointment. Of course, you may feel free to call me any time.

Sincerely,

Alicia Agent

Alicia Agent

Figure 9.5 Direct Mail Letter to FSBOs — Form of Letter

Golden Threshold Realty, Inc.

1515 Marigold Centre Drive, New Wabash, West Carolina 01010

From the Desk of *Alan Agent*, REALTOR®

FIELD [NAME]
FIELD [CITY/STATE] FIELD [ZIP]

Dear FIELD [NAME]:

Congratulations on your decision to sell your home! I have begun a unique program to assist people like you who are selling their own property. FIELD [NAME], while I respect your decision to market your home yourself, I know how much work it can be. I'd like to offer you the following services:

- All the legal forms you'll need to complete a sale;
- Referrals to all the best escrow, title, insurance, property protection, property inspection, lending and termite companies;
- A telephone consultation with the top real estate agent in FIELD [CITY];
- If you are relocating, a referral to the top agents in any city in the U.S.

In return, I'd ask only that you forward to me the names and phone numbers of only those people who do not buy your house; referrals to anyone you know who may be interested in buying or selling property in our community; and the names and phone numbers of anyone who needs to sell their own property before they can buy yours.

I'd also ask that you permit me to make a presentation of my marketing services in the event you decide to list your property with an agent.

I hope you'll appreciate this low-pressure attempt to do a little mutual back-scratching. You may call me or my staff if you're interested in these materials or services. I've enclosed a simple form to keep track of potential clientele, and a brochure on selling your own home.

Thank you in advance for what I think will be a profitable partnership!

Sincerely,

SUMMARY

The purpose of advertising is to get the agent's name into the marketplace, so the public will make a mental connection between the agent's name and the idea of a successful and efficient real estate professional. Three main print advertising strategies most often used by assistants are brochures, newsletters and direct mailings.

An effective brochure will be visually interesting, with good graphic design. A photograph of the agent should be a recognizable likeness of the agent's everyday appearance. Information in a brochure should be factual and brief.

A newsletter is a tool for providing information to readers while at the same time marketing the agent's services. Newsletters should contain a mix of news and marketing articles.

Direct mail involves sending personalized letters to specific target markets. Word processing software permits easy and effective merging of names and addresses into a form letter.

KEY TERMS

bi-fold
merged file
brochure
newsletter
direct mail
personalized

farm
primary file
field
secondary file
fliers
tri-fold

font
typeface
mail-merge
visual interest
mass mailing

Review Questions

1. Assistant *T* created a tri-fold marketing piece on heavy, glossy paper. It featured her agent's accomplishments and skills in bullet-point lists, accompanied by photos of the agent at work. This marketing piece was most likely a

   a. newsletter.
   b. brochure.
   c. direct mail letter.
   d. display ad.

2. "Visual interest" refers to

   a. good graphic design.
   b. informative text.
   c. the agent's photograph.
   d. a newsletter's headline.

3. An agent's photo should be included in a brochure

   a. because agents like to see their pictures in print.
   b. because it's an opportunity for the agent to have a glamorous photo taken.
   c. so that people can associate a face with the name.
   d. so that the assistant needs to write less.

4. The text of a brochure should *not* include

   a. quotes from satisfied former clients.
   b. the agent's real estate background.
   c. long paragraphs about the agent's life.
   d. bullet-pointed lists of accomplishments.

5. Which of the following formats is usually *not* used for newsletters?

   a. Bi-fold
   b. Single page
   c. Multipage
   d. Tri-fold

6. An article with the headline, "New Tax Law Makes It Smart to Sell!" is best classified as a

   a. news-type article in a newsletter.
   b. marketing-type article in a newsletter.
   c. bullet-point topic in a brochure.
   d. first paragraph in a direct mail letter.

7. Direct mail is sending a

   a. single letter to one individual only.
   b. form letter to "Dear Homeowner."
   c. personalized form letter to multiple recipients in a target market.
   d. identical letters or brochures to multiple recipients in a targeted market.

8. *𝒫* and **P** are examples of different

   a. graphic designs.
   b. typefaces.
   c. letters.
   d. formats.

9. Your agent comes to you and says, "A new company is relocating 300 workers to town. Here's a list of their names. What should we do?" The most effective marketing technique in this situation would be:

   a. Create a brochure to hand out to the relocaters when the visit the office.
   b. Generate a direct-mail letter to send out to the relocaters.
   c. Write an article about the relocation for the agent's newsletter.
   d. Have a billboard ad set up near the airport.

10. In Figure 9.5, which of the following would be most likely to be inserted in the *fifth* field?

    a. Robert Smith
    b. Mr. Robert Smith
    c. Mr. Smith
    d. Bob

10

Assisting With Sellers

In this chapter, we will examine the real estate assistant's supportive role in helping the agent sell a property, from the listing presentation through showings and open houses to helping prepare the purchase offer and coordinating the closing.

Closing and escrow are discussed in detail in Chapter 12, and the purchase and sale agreement is examined in Chapter 11 on buyers. This chapter focuses on the assistant's role in the agent's relationship with the seller. By the end of the chapter, you should be able to identify the preparations necessary for a listing presentation, and understand how to prepare a competitive market analysis (CMA). You will also be able to outline the important basic steps in marketing a property.

THE SALES SUPPORT ROLE

A licensed assistant may act as the agent's direct support person in the sales process by participating in most of the important aspects of a selling-side transaction:

- ❖ preparation of materials for listing presentation
- ❖ preparation of competitive market analysis (CMA)
- ❖ preparation of home brochure and other handouts
- ❖ assisting with showings and agent previews
- ❖ arranging open houses
- ❖ keeping track of listing activity

This **sales support** role is one of the assistant's most important jobs. A licensed assistant can take an active role in sales support activities, including assisting the agent in conducting negotiations.

An unlicensed assistant can act as an indirect sales support professional by handling all the paperwork, production, errands and miscellaneous office details that need to be taken care of, freeing the agent for sales activities.

PRE-LISTING SALES SUPPORT

The **pre-listing phase** is extremely important. This is the time when the marketing strategies pay off by producing a potential client. The trick now is to convince the potential client to become an actual client by signing a listing agreement (discussed in Chapter 1). Turning a potential client into an actual one is a delicate operation that requires skill, sensitivity and preparation. The agent is successful for two reasons: he or she can attract listings and sell them. The pre-listing phase is the agent's opportunity to display his or her professional skills by convincing the sellers to entrust their home sale to him or her. That decision is a delicate one for most home sellers. They want an agent who can be a ruthless "shark" with potential buyers (without scaring them away). At the same time, sellers want an agent whom they can trust with intimate personal information and the key to their house. Most sellers also want to like their agent, too. As a result, the agent has to be a ferocious carnivore, a pillar of the community, and a good ol' buddy all wrapped up in one competent professional. That takes a lot of effort, and it's the assistant's job to give the agent the necessary time and flexibility.

Prepping the Sellers

The assistant is often the potential client's first point of contact with the agent. In previous chapters, we've discussed various strategies for the assistant to create a good first impression with potential clients. There is also another important job for the licensed assistant at this time: preparing (or "**prepping**") the sellers for the agent's listing presentation.

The agent will need certain information from the sellers in order to make an effective and meaningful presentation. Rather than have the agent conduct a pre-presentation interview, the assistant can obtain the necessary information from the sellers over the phone or in a personal meeting. Figure 10.1 illustrates a pre-listing questionnaire containing the questions assistants most frequently need to ask potential sellers. Figure 10.2 is a pre-listing presentation checklist.

I have a lot of listing presentations to do, and it really helps when my assistant does the preliminary legwork for me. Nothing's worse than going into a presentation "cold," knowing very little about the sellers.

Listing Presentation Book

Earlier in this book, we discussed listing packets — envelopes or file folders that contain all the forms and documents an agent needs to list a home — as organizing tools. Related to the listing packet is the **listing presentation book**: a printed marketing tool the agent uses to emphasize his or her oral presentation.

Figure 10.1 Pre-Listing Questionnaire

Property Address				
Date of Call	Caller		Call Taken By	
Sellers Name(s)				
Mailing Address				
Phone Number(s) Home			Work	
How did you hear about us?				
Referral:				
Reason for selling:				
APPOINTMENT TIME:				
Persons who will be present:				
Interviewing other agents? Yes No Names:				
Other properties owned				
Selling them, too? Yes No				
Where are you moving?				
Do you know of an agent there?				
Desired sale date				
Purchase price paid $	Owned how long?			
Property Type	Sq. Ft. (int)	Sq. Ft. (ext)	Other Amenities	Income Property
Total Rooms	Basement	School Dist		Lease
Bedrooms	AC	Garage		Rent
Baths	Deck/Porch	Appliances		Tenants?
NOTES:				

Figure 10.2 Pre-Listing Presentation Checklist

FORMS	
Authorization to Sell	
Listing Agreement	
Agency Disclosure	
CMA	
Seller's Net Analysis	
Lockbox permission	
Permission to post sign	
MLS property data form	
MATERIALS	
Presentation Book	
Personalized Presentation Folder	
Videotape	
Laptop Computer	
SUPPLIES	
Pens	
Scratch pads	
Business cards	
Calculator	
Measuring tape	

While the listing presentation book is a print-based marketing tool, assistants should be aware that a growing number of real estate agents are turning to electronic media, such as videotapes and on-line services or computer software to augment their presentations. A video with high production values (such as background music, professional editing and use of animation or graphics) can be an effective tool for the high-tech agent.

The listing book is typically a three-ring binder with pages containing:

- sample newspaper advertisements for homes
- photographs illustrating marketing techniques such as signs, open house displays and televised advertisement
- personal marketing materials about the agent, such as his or her brochures or newsletters
- letters of reference or recommendation
- information about the forms of agency available
- the agent's vision statement
- a statement on the advantages of listing with a licensed real estate agent
- a history of the office
- information about the services available, such as relocation counseling, financial advice or other services
- an explanation of how multiple-listing services work
- other materials the agent believes would be helpful in illustrating his or her presentation
- a pocket containing pamphlets and informative brochures the agent may distribute to prospective sellers, such as his or her own brochure or NAR publications, such as "Selling Your Home" or "Moving Made Easy"

The use of color and a mix of text and illustrations is important, because the package is a visual marketing tool: prospective sellers will be looking at it at the same time they are listening to the agent. The book should be updated frequently to ensure that it's current. The advantage of the three-ring binder format is that alternative or replacement pages may be easily integrated.

...FOR EXAMPLE

This week, Agent G has listing presentations with: (1) a couple who is retiring and planning a move to a warmer climate; (2) an executor who is selling his deceased aunt's home; and (3) an owner who is selling her three-unit apartment building. Agent G's assistant prepares some special pages for the presentation book. One lists the agent's relocation services, with emphasis on contacts in Florida and Arizona. A second page features inexpensive fix-up tips for vacant homes, while a third lists the responsibilities of executors with regard to selling real estate; a fourth page lists the agent's past sales of income properties. The pages may be put into the book and taken out easily, depending on which presentation is being given. That way, Agent G will not have to say, "That page isn't relevant," but can focus on the services that directly concern the seller. In addition, G's presentation will be more effective because it will be tailored to the individual interests of each seller.

Competitive Market Analysis (CMA)

One of the most important issues that will arise during the listing presentation is price: how much to ask for the property. The sellers will probably have a price in mind, some figure that will permit them to recover their investment in the property (initial purchase plus improvements) and realize a profit sufficient to meet their needs for whatever their next transaction will be: the purchase of a newer, larger home, for instance, or investment for retirement. Often times, however, the seller's original notion of how much to ask for his or her property does not reflect the reality of the local real estate market.

It is important to remember, however, that it is the seller who decides the property's price. *A real estate agent may never tell a seller what price to ask for a property.* Nonetheless, it is the responsibility of the broker or salesperson to advise and assist the seller in determining the listing price. Because the average seller does not usually have the background to make an informed decision about a reasonable listing price, real estate agents must be prepared to offer their knowledge, information and expertise.

A broker or salesperson can help the seller determine a listing price by using a **competitive market analysis (CMA)**. A CMA is a comparison of the prices of recently sold properties that are similar in location, style and amenities to the listing seller's property. *A CMA is not a formal appraisal.* In many states, only a licensed appraiser can offer a property appraisal. A CMA is simply a comparison of one property to other, similar properties based on shared qualities. The purpose of a CMA is to determine the property's **market value**: the most probable price property would bring in an arm's-length transaction between a willing seller and buyer under normal conditions in the open market. Obviously, the property's actual **market price** won't be known until an offer is made and accepted. The market price is the same as the selling price, because the selling price reflects the value placed on the property by the market. The market price may or may not be the same as the projected market value.

At the prelisting presentation, the agent can give the seller an accurate estimate of the price the seller's property is likely to bring under current market conditions, based on the past performance of similar properties. Because "how much will I get?" is the big question for sellers, the agent must be prepared to offer a realistic estimate. An agent who promises enormous profits without regard to the market is setting the stage for a disappointed client: the sales process will last for many months, and the inflated price will not be offered. On the other hand, an agent who greatly underestimates a property's market value will probably have a quick sale, but the seller may be unsatisfied. The agent's commission, of course, is included in the listing price, and must also be taken into consideration.

The assistant's role in preparing the CMA is to gather the relevant information into a convenient package for the agent. Ultimately, it is the agent who must determine the market value of any property, but the assistant plays a vital role by gathering the data and performing the research.

The assistant will need to obtain the following:

- the PIN (property identification number) of the property
- a plat map indicating the exact dimensions of the property and structures
- the property's location on a city or neighborhood map, indicating the exact neighborhood or area, school districts and transportation
- property information required for an MLS input form
- comparable properties sold within the past six months
- comparables with pending sales (some agents also use expired listings), listed within the past six to eight months
- comparable properties currently for sale, listed within the past six to eight months.

In the past, this information would have been compiled in a large stack of photocopies of MLS pages, maps and files. Today, computer programs are available both independently and through a local MLS that will find comparable properties within whatever search parameters are selected. Based on such considerations as location, square footage and special features, the computer will generate a "comp" form in minutes. The list of comparable properties can be made longer or shorter by changing the listing date parameters (the older the listings, the longer the list of comparables) or the comparable qualities. Obviously, the more generic the comparable properties, the more listings the computer will find; however a CMA is more valuable the more the comparables are similar to the property being valued.

The assistant may also need to prepare a CMA presentation folder. Some agents like to present prospective sellers with personalized folder containing the comparable properties, a list of elements used to determine the suggested range of asking prices, and a breakdown of the seller's return based on a median asking price.

MARKETING THE PROPERTY

The assistant plays an active role in marketing a property once it's listed with the agent. In his or her capacity as an active sales support person, the assistant will have continuous and frequent contact with sellers. During the sales phase of a real estate transaction, the seller is under constant emotional pressure: the tension of keeping a house tidy and presentable; the worry over whether or not a buyer will be found; the annoyance of having to vacate the property every time a showing is scheduled; the excitement of looking for a new home or planning a move — the tension-creating factors are numerous and intense. Frequently, the seller's emotional anxiety is the assistant's direct concern: irate or nervous phone calls to the agent need to be fielded with sensitivity and efficiency. The agent is obliged to maintain regular contact with the client, to keep the client informed of activity and offers. However, there may be problems or complications that the assistant is capable of dealing with, rather than burdening the agent with more work. The assistant needs to have a positive attitude regardless of the seller's attitude, and must try to reassure the client that the agent has the situation under control.

It is important that the assistant establish a relationship with each client. The agent will mention his or her assistant's role during the presentation (some agents prefer to be accompanied by an assistant as well). The assistant should contact the seller independently, with a note or phone call, so that the seller feels comfortable dealing with the assistant, and will not insist on speaking directly to the agent on all issues.

In addition to the assistant's role in calming worried clients, there are several concrete chores that must be performed during the sales period:

- ❖ A *"for sale" sign* must be placed on the property, if allowed by local laws (see Chapter 4).
- ❖ A *lockbox* must be installed on the door (see Chapter 4).
- ❖ A *photograph* must be taken of the property (see Chapter 5), to be included in MLS books, displayed in the office, and used for newspaper advertisements.
- ❖ A ***home marketing flier*** must be produced that advertises the home's character, such as location, size, number of rooms, style and age. The flier should feature information about new appliances, special amenities or attractive qualities such as décor, large rooms, woodwork details or a security system. The flier should prominently display the agent's name and phone number. Information regarding price, taxes and utility bills should also be included.
- ❖ A ***financing flier*** must be produced that discusses mortgage interest rates, qualifying incomes required for different mortgage amounts, and detailing the terms of any seller-financing available.
- ❖ Showings and previews must be scheduled. A **showing** is when an agent brings a potential buyer through the property. A **preview**, on the other hand, is when an agent views the property without bringing a buyer. The listing agent may want to hold an **agents' open house**, which is an opportunity for other agents from the same office, or other interested agents, to preview the property. For an agent's open house, the assistant will need to mail or fax invitations to the other agents, and arrange for refreshments (such as coffee and cookies) and door prizes. The more agents who look at a property, the more likely it is to sell quickly. The agent's office may hold its own weekly **agents' tour** of new listings.

Open House

The assistant plays an important role in ensuring that an open house is a successful marketing event. There are a number of preliminary planning steps that must be taken, and the assistant is responsible for ensuring that important items are present on the day of the open house.

In some offices, a licensed assistant may be asked to host the open house. Under the law of some states, an unlicensed assistant may be present at an open house, and may distribute marketing materials, but may not provide independent information or assist prospective buyers in preparing an offer.

First, the assistant needs to make sure that an advertisement for the open house is submitted to local newspapers before the paper's deadline. The ad should appear as close to the open house date as possible. Where the newspaper is distributed in the morning, the ad should appear that day, too.

Deadlines and prices can be obtained from a newspaper's classified advertising department. It is a good idea to establish a positive working relationship with the people in the classified department — you can never tell when you might need to ask a favor. Ads should be submitted in whatever format the paper requires well before the deadline. You should establish a reputation for being on time and not creating extra work.

Before the open house, the assistant should:

- obtain the owner's permission — the open house should be held on a convenient day and time for the owner, as well as dictated by marketing considerations
- print extra copies of the home marketing flier and financing flier
- obtain a plat of the property, blueprints, the seller's statement of condition, and information about the neighborhood, schools and community
- collect copies of the agent's marketing brochure and business cards, along with printouts of the agent's other listings, and put them in a box along with the fliers, plat, blueprints, seller's statement and other materials
- send out announcements of the open house to other agents

An open house checklist appears in Figure 10.3.

On the day of the open house, the assistant should:

- place "open house" directional signs around the neighborhood, and an open house sign in front of the property
- if the agent requests, place streamers, banners or balloons in front of the property
- bring a guest register and open house survey (see Figure 10.4) to the open house, along with the fliers, agent brochure and business cards and other boxed materials
- if refreshments are being served, remember to bring them, along with cups, napkins, condiments and utensils
- check the home's condition for cleanliness, clutter and lighting: rooms should be bright and well-ventilated, and burnt-out light bulbs should be replaced

After the open house, the assistant should:

- ❖ leave a note reviewing the open house: how many visitors, common reactions, suggestions to improve the home's showing appeal, etc.
- ❖ remove litter and trash
- ❖ make sure the home is in the same condition as before the open house
- ❖ remove the extra yard signs, decorations and directional signs
- ❖ prepare a list of follow-up calls to make to anyone who signed the guest register, completed a survey or left a business card

TRACKING SALES ACTIVITY

Sellers always want to know what their agent is doing to earn his or her commission. The best and most convincing way to reassure sellers that their agent is doing his or her job is to keep a record of all sales activities regarding each listed property. In addition to helping the agent make accurate regular reports to clients, the **sales activity log** also provides a good signal for when to make price or marketing strategy changes for a particular property.

The sales activity log should include the date, time and number of telephone calls:

- ❖ generated by a newspaper advertisement
- ❖ from other agents
- ❖ from people who drove by the property and saw the sign

The log should also include the dates when:

- ❖ advertisements were placed in local papers
- ❖ open houses were held, and the number of visitors
- ❖ the property was shown by the listing agent
- ❖ the property was shown by another agent

Figure 10.3 Open House Checklist

Open House Address: ______________________________

Date: ____________ Attending: ______________, Agent ____________, Assistant

<table>
<tr><th colspan="7">PRELIMINARIES</th></tr>
<tr><td colspan="3">Notify Owner</td><td colspan="4">Invitations sent</td></tr>
<tr><td colspan="3">Key arrangements</td><td colspan="4">"Open House Tips" brochure to Owner</td></tr>
<tr><td>Ad in ___________</td><td colspan="2">Submitted: ___/___/___</td><td>To Appear: ___/___/___</td><td>OK</td><td></td><td>Problem:</td></tr>
<tr><td>Ad in ___________</td><td colspan="2">Submitted: ___/___/___</td><td>To Appear: ___/___/___</td><td>OK</td><td></td><td>Problem:</td></tr>
<tr><td colspan="7">Notes:</td></tr>
</table>

OPEN HOUSE BOX				
Home marketing flier		Seller statement		Other:
Financing flier		Tax/Utilities		
Agent brochure		Area Info		
Listing		Other listings		
Business cards		Qualifier forms		
Guest register		Purchase & sale		
Surveys				
Plans/Plat				

MATERIALS				
Yard Sign		Directionals		Other:
Refreshments		Decorations		
Cups, napkins		Scratch pads		
Calculator		Laptop		

CLEAN UP				
Activity report		Signs removed		Notes:
Follow-up list				
Housecleaning				

Figure 10.4 Open House Survey

Golden Threshold Realty, Inc.

"25 Years of Bringing People Home"

Thank you for attending today's Open House at 619 Pleasant Street.
Please take a moment to fill out this questionnaire before you leave . . .

Name: ______________________________

Address: ______________________________

Home Phone: ______________ Work Phone: ______________

How did you find out about this home?

Newspaper Mailing Sign Other______________

Are you currently selling or planning to sell your home? Yes No

What did you like *most* about this home? ______________

____

What did you like *least* about this home? ______________

____

I would like more information about this home or other properties. Please call me.

Yes ____ No, not at this time ____

The sellers appreciate your time and honesty in answering these questions. If I can help you in any of your real estate needs, please don't hesitate to contact me.

Betty Broker — Golden Threshold Realty

SUMMARY

A licensed assistant may act as the agent's direct support person by participating in a variety of sales-related activities. The pre-listing phase is an extremely important time, when the potential client is convinced to become an actual client. The assistant is often the potential client's first point of contact with the agent.

The assistant prepares an agent's listing presentation book, which supports and emphasizes the agent's listing presentation. The assistant also helps prepare a competitive market analysis.

Once property is listed with an agent, the assistant plays a very active role in marketing the property by dealing with seller concerns, tracking sales and marketing activity, preparing (and, in some cases conducting) open houses, and dealing with the details of real estate marketing such as signs, fliers and advertising.

It is important to keep careful track of all marketing activities for each property.

KEY TERMS

agents' open house
agents' tour
competitive market analysis (CMA)
financing flier
listing presentation book
market price
market value
home marketing flier
pre-listing phase
prepping
preview
sales support
sales activity log
showing

Review Questions

1. Which of the following activities would *not* be included as a "sales support" activity?

    a. Preparing materials for a listing presentation
    b. Tracking listing activities
    c. Designing an agent's marketing brochure
    d. Designing a home marketing brochure

2. Which of the following activities is *not* part of pre-listing sales support?

    a. Prepping the property owners
    b. Assembling a listing presentation book
    c. Preparing a CMA
    d. Scheduling an open house

3. A listing presentation book is

    a. an envelope or file folder that contains all the forms an documents needed to list a home.
    b. typically a three-ring binder of materials used to emphasize and support an oral listing presentation.
    c. essentially the same as a competitive market analysis.
    d. one of the materials an assistant must be sure to include in an open house box.

4. *CMA* stands for

    a. competitive market analysis.
    b. complete market analysis.
    c. competitor's marketing analysis.
    d. competing market analysis.

5. *Market value* is the

    a. owner's asking price.
    b. listing price selected by the agent.
    c. actual selling price.
    d. estimate of the probable selling price.

6. Which of the following is required to prepare a good CMA?

    a. The seller's name
    b. Comps
    c. A folder
    d. Illustrations

7. A home marketing flier

    a. discusses mortgage interest rates and qualifying incomes.
    b. emphasizes the agent's record of successful selling.
    c. should not mention the listing price of the property.
    d. advertises the home's character, features and special amenities.

8. On May 15, Agent *N* took Agent *C* to walk through a condominium *N* had recently listed. On May 17, *C* brought a prospective buyer to walk through the condominium. Which of the following statements is true?

    a. The May 15 visit was a *preview*; the May 17 visit was a *listing*.
    b. The May 15 visit was a *showing*; the May 17 visit was a *preview*.
    c. The May 15 visit was a *preview*; the May 17 visit was a *showing*.
    d. Both visits were *showings*.

9. Which of the following should an assistant *not* do before an open house?

    a. Obtain the owner's permission
    b. Send out invitations
    c. Gather information about the community
    d. Prepare a list of follow-up calls

10. A method of tracking sales activity by recording all sales- and marketing-related events involving a particular property is a

    a. sales activity log.
    b. market activity log.
    c. CMA.
    d. MLS.

11

Assisting With Buyers

In this chapter, we will discuss the assistant's role in dealing with buyers, both as the agent's customers and as clients. As the real estate market changes, and as consumers become more sophisticated, buyers are expecting a different and higher degree of service.

By the end of the chapter, you should be able to identify the services appropriate to both buyer-customers and buyer-clients, and apply the methods of screening buyers and focusing buyer interest. You should also understand the requirements and processes involved in preparing an offer and a purchase agreement.

TYPES OF BUYERS

There are essentially three types of buyers in the real estate world: focused buyers, browsers and window shoppers. Later in this chapter we'll consider the assistant's role when his or her agent is a buyer's broker and the buyers are clients. The three basic types are the agent's customers: that is, the broker or salesperson is the agent of the seller (see Chapter 1).

1. **Focused buyers** are buyers who have found a specific property they want to buy, or who know within a few blocks the area in which they want to live. They have a clear understanding of their financial capabilities and of the type of properties that are available.

2. **Browsers**, on the other hand, are serious buyers who know generally what they want, but who have not yet decided exactly what sort of property best meets their needs. Eventually, after they've looked at a number of properties and have made some decisions, browsers will become focused buyers.

3. The third type of buyer isn't really a buyer at all. There are people whose idea of a fun Sunday afternoon is being chauffeured around town by a real estate agent, looking at other people's houses. While some of these "**window shoppers**" will eventually evolve into browsers and finally into focused buyers, many do not. They are a continuing nuisance to agents.

It's an important part of an assistant's job to be able to discriminate among these three types of buyers, and to weed out the ones who are not yet ready to commit to home ownership. At the same time, even the most time-wasting window shopper may eventually become a browser or focused buyer; the assistant must be able to add these people to the farm (see Chapter 9).

BUYERS AS CUSTOMERS

When an agent represents sellers, the people who buy his or her client's property are the agent's customers. In Chapter 1, we discussed the various types of agency relationships, and the duties owed by agents to their customers.

Just as the assistant is often the potential seller's first point of contact with the agent, the assistant is the first contact a prospective buyer will have with the agent as well. As mentioned above, it is at this point that the effective assistant will be able to determine what sort of buyer has come into the office, what his or her needs are, and what to do.

Everyone's a Buyer

An assistant should assume that anyone who calls about a property is a serious buyer. It is an unfortunate fact of life, of course, that many phone calls will be from curious neighbors or FSBOs engaging in market research. Nonetheless, the assistant who is screening calls for the agent cannot know with any certainty how serious the caller may be. Similarly, when people come into the office in person (referred to as **walk-ins**), it is dangerous to make assumptions based on their appearance.

People hardly ever put on their best clothes to go visit a real estate agent, I'm sorry to say. I always warn my assistants not to make any assumptions about people based on their clothing. Some very well-to-do people "dress down" on the weekends. I also remind assistants that discriminating on any basis can come dangerously close to breaking the law. So we have a big rule in my office: *Never Assume, Because You'll Make an "Ass-" of "-U-" and "-Me"!*

Pre-Qualification

The only way to accurately determine whether a person is a willing and able buyer is to ask them. In many offices, buyers are asked to complete a **buyer information sheet** (see Figure 11.1). It's unlikely that a window shopper will want to take the time to fill it out, or will want to disclose the information necessary to be prequalified. **Prequalification** is the process by which a prospective buyer's ability to purchase a given property may be determined. The prequalification form uses general income, savings, debt and credit-worthiness information to determine the price-range of homes the individual can afford. The agent may also use the interviewing process to learn more about the buyer's ability and willingness to assume the responsibilities of home ownership.

Thorough prequalification saves the agent a lot of time wasted showing prospective buyers properties they cannot afford. A licensed assistant may be responsible for conducting pre-qualification interviews or assisting the agent in prequalifying buyers.

Buyer Profiles

There are other ways for the screening assistant to determine the prospective buyer's level of interest and what he or she is looking for:

- ***Did the prospective buyer respond to a newspaper ad for a particular property?*** If so, the individual is already looking with some degree of seriousness. He or she is spending time reading the real estate advertisements, and has taken the initiative to call on specific properties. The prospective buyer already has an idea of what he or she wants and what he or she can afford. This person is probably a fairly focused browser.

- ***Did the prospective buyer respond to a general advertisement for the agent's services?*** If so, the individual is likely to be a browser: someone who has decided he or she wants to buy, but who doesn't have a clear idea yet about any special property.

- ***Did the prospective buyer call or walk in?*** This is a strong indicator of seriousness. A telephone (even in these days of caller i.d.) provides a caller with a certain degree of anonymity: he or she can get the information and hang up without leaving his or her name. While many callers are serious buyers, a person who comes to an agent's office in person may be somewhat more eager. An individual who makes a personal visit is saying, in effect, "I want to sit down with a real estate professional and discuss my situation." It's like the difference between calling a doctor's office for free medical advice and walking into the clinic.

- ***Is the prospective buyer willing to fill out the information sheet and be prequalified?*** Like telephone-anonymity, even a person who walks into a real estate office can still walk out without leaving a name or number. Once the prospective buyers have filled out the form, however, and sat down with the agent or assistant to disclose their personal finances, they have committed themselves to giving the home buying decision serious consideration.

Of course, some prospective buyers will come into a real estate office prepared to make an offer on a specific property that day. Those days are nice, but rare.

Other Buyer Services

In Chapter 5 we discussed the buyer packet: a folder containing information the agent will want to present to prospective buyers. The packet usually contains marketing materials about the agent and the real estate services offered, about agency issues, and about the community.

Figure 11.1 Buyer Information Sheet

PERSONAL INFORMATION

Name(s):________________________________

Current Address: ________________________________

Phone Number: (Home) ________________ (Work) ________________

(Home) ________________ (Work) ________________

Currently Owns Home? YES NO Planning to Sell Before Buying? YES NO

Currently Represented by Broker? YES NO Broker: ____________________

HOME BUYING CRITERIA

Geographical Area(s):

1. ________________________ 2. ________________________

Type of Property:

□ single family □ single family (w/income) □ multi-unit □ condominium □ townhouse
□ other:

Size Requirements:

□ 1 bedroom □ 2 bedroom □ 3 bedroom □ 4+ bedroom □ 1 bath □ 1.5 bath
□ 2 bath □ 2.5 bath □ basement □ large yard □ small yard □ garage
□ Other: ____________

Preferences:

□ single-family □ condo □ single-storey □ 2+ □ split level □ high-rise
□ security □ handicapped accessible □ low floor □ high floor □ quiet
□ brick □ frame □ aluminum □ stucco □ Cape Cod □ Georgian
□ colonial □ modern □ near school □ near shopping □ near transit
□ other: ________________________________

PRELIMINARY FINANCIAL INFORMATION

Price Range: $________________________ Financing:____________________

Down Payment: $________________ Source of Down Payment: ________________

Current Mortgage? YES NO Amount Borrowed/Owed: $________ /$________

Some agents use the listing packet for both sellers and buyers, while others have a special buyers packet available. The buyers packet is most often sent out to out of town buyers before they arrive to look at properties, but may also be distributed to local buyers as well.

An assistant's responsibilities toward a buyer-customer include:

- locating listings that correspond to the buyer's preferences and price range
- scheduling showings of properties
- keeping the agent informed about the buyer's interests and responses to properties
- maintaining a file record on the buyer, including the buyer information form, prequalification materials, and records of showings (see Figure 11.2). This file will become an important part of the agent's farm, both for finding buyers and for future cultivation as a seller.

Once a buyer has made an offer on a property, and the offer has been accepted by the seller, the assistant may be asked to help the buyer arrange for property inspections and a mortgage application. The buyer may seek assistance with arranging a move and finding decorators or tradespeople. Remember: the closing depends on the buyer's loan approval, so assisting the buyer with financing arrangements helps make the transaction possible. In addition, today's buyer may well be tomorrow's seller, so establishing a good relationship now will be likely to pay off later.

BUYERS AS CLIENTS

Many agents today are acting as representatives for purchasers (see Chapter 1). While the basic services a buyer will expect of a buyer's agent are the same as a buyer-customer would receive (finding compatible listings, being shown properties, being assisted with an offer and pre-closing matters such as financing and moving), the relationship is based on a contract that establishes an agency arrangement. That means that the agent owes the buyer the traditional agency duties of care, obedience, accounting, loyalty and disclosure (see Chapter 1). The buyer may be expected to pay the agent a fee for the agent's services, or the agent may be paid a commission based on the sales price of the property, depending on the type of agreement used in a particular office.

One advantage of working with a buyer's broker is that there is little need to screen buyers for seriousness: if they've sought out a buyer's broker, and are willing to sign an agency agreement, they're serious about buying.

Buyer's Broker Services

While both seller's and buyer's brokers will arrange for property showings, assist buyers with financing arrangements, provide accurate information about a property, explain the forms and agreements used and monitor the closing process, a buyer's broker performs additional services on the buyer's behalf. An assistant to a buyer's broker will need to be aware of these additional services, because they will be an important part of his or her job.

The additional buyer's broker services are:

- *Prepare a property value study.* A **property value study (PVS)** is similar to a CMA, but assembled from the perspective of the buyer. That is, the ultimate goal of a CMA is to determine the maximum price a seller is likely to get for his or her property. The goal of a PVS, on the other hand, is to determine the lowest amount a buyer should have to pay for a property. A PVS, then, will focus on the narrowest comparisons, and take into account expenses likely to be incurred to repair or update a property. *A PVS is not a formal appraisal.* The PVS is often used to justify a lower-than-asking price based on how a particular property *fails* to compare favorably with its CMA comparables, and the costs the buyer is likely to have to incur in order to make necessary improvements. The assistant may need to gather and analyze comps with a more critical eye.

- *Maintain confidentiality.* A seller's agent is not obligated to keep financial and bargaining information obtained from a buyer confidential; in fact, the seller's agent is obliged to pass on such information to the seller. A buyer's agent (and his or her assistant) *must keep the buyer's financial situation and bargaining posture strictly confidential.*

- *Point out negatives.* Any agent is responsible for disclosing known material defects in a property. However, a buyer's agent may also discuss other factors with the buyer: a less-than-ideal location, for instance, or an awkward floor plan.

- *Know the market.* The buyer's agent is responsible for finding out useful information about the sellers. If the agent knows that the sellers are desperate to move, for instance, the buyer will want to know.

- *Negotiate on the buyer's behalf.* The buyer's agent will help the buyer write an offer and negotiate a sale with the buyer's interests in mind: a lower price, lower down payment, more favorable financing or closing conditions.

THE PURCHASE AGREEMENT

The whole real estate sales process comes down to two things: the closing, which concludes the transaction (see Chapter 12), and the **purchase agreement**, which makes the closing possible. Purchase and sale agreements, and offers to purchase, are generally prepared on a standard, pre-printed blank form. The forms may be provided by the local association of REALTORS®, by a local legal stationers, or they may be designed and printed especially for an individual real estate office. An assistant needs to be totally familiar with the forms used in his or her area, as well as with the forms used by his or her office. In the case of new construction, builders and developers usually have their own purchase agreement forms, and different forms are used for land sales and commercial transactions.

Figure 11.2 Buyer Showing Sheet

As we look at homes today, please use this form to record your responses. It will help you remember the distinguishing features of each home, and will help me understand more clearly exactly what you're looking for.

Buyer Name: ______________________________ Date of Showing: __________

PROPERTY DESCRIPTION: ***Address and Features***	***OPINION***
	Positives: Negatives: Interest: □High □ Moderate □ Low □ None
	Positives: Negatives: Interest: □High □ Moderate □ Low □ None
	Positives: Negatives: Interest: □High □ Moderate □ Low □ None

It is important to note the process by which a purchase and sale agreement is finalized. The buyer first makes an offer to the seller. The seller then has three options: he or she may:

1. *accept* the offer exactly as it was made by the buyer; or
2. *reject* the offer; or
3. make a *counteroffer*: this is actually a rejection of the first offer. The seller is, in effect, making a new offer to the buyer. The buyer may then accept the counteroffer, reject the counteroffer, or counter it with a new offer, starting the whole process over again.

This process of multiple offers and counteroffers is known as *negotiation*; it's also a process that often means a long night for the agent (and the assistant) who has to shuttle back and forth between the parties to present offers and counteroffers until either an agreement is reached or the deal falls through because the parties cannot agree to terms.

Purchase and Sale Agreement Checklist

Once an agreement is reached, and the purchase and sale agreement has been signed by both the buyer and the seller, the assistant's work has just begun. The first thing to be dealt with is the buyer's earnest money.

It is customary for a purchaser to provide a deposit, usually in the form of a check, when making an offer to purchase real estate. The amount is generally no more than 10 percent of the purchase price. This deposit is commonly referred to as an **earnest money** check (also known as a *binder*, *initial deposit*, *bargain money* and a *good-faith deposit*). Its purpose is to show the buyer's good faith intention to carry out the terms of the offer. It says, in effect, "I'm in earnest." The check is given to the listing broker at the time the contract is signed, to be held in a special escrow account on behalf of the seller. Once the sale goes to closing, the money is released from the account and paid over to the seller, with any interest it earned being paid back to the purchaser, unless the agreement calls for some other distribution.

State law strictly regulates how the earnest money is handled by the broker. Basically, the broker must maintain a special bank account just for earnest money deposits and may never **commingle** — that is, mix together — earnest money deposits with his or her own funds. Commingling of funds is always grounds for discipline, and may include the loss of the broker's license and criminal prosecution. Because a licensed assistant may be called upon to process earnest money checks, assistants should be clearly aware of their office's policies and procedures, as well as state law, regarding how earnest money deposits are handled.

The checklist in Figure 11.3 outlines the issues that must be dealt with immediately after the purchase and sale agreement is finalized. Once these initial matters have been taken care of, the assistant can concentrate on making sure the deal goes to closing: a process discussed in the next chapter.

Figure 11.3 Purchase and Sale Agreement / Pre-Closing Checklist

□ Deposit earnest money check number _________ □ Receipt to client

PROOFREAD AGREEMENT

Are all terms clearly specified? Yes No
Is the purchase price specified? Yes No
Is property clearly identified? Yes No
Buyers identified? Yes No
Sellers identified? Yes No
Is the down payment specified? Yes No
Are financing terms specified? Yes No
Closing date? Yes No

All blanks filled in or lined out? Yes No
All signatures on signature lines? Yes No
___Buyers ___Sellers
___Agent (Buyer) ___Agent (Seller)
Changes or additions initialed? Yes No

CONTINGENCIES: Home inspection by _________ Contingency lifted by _________
Loan qualification by _________ Attorney review by _________

"Contract Pending" sign □ Update transaction file □ Report sale to MLS □

ESCROW Name of officer _______________ □ **CLOSED**
Company _______________
Address _______________
Phone _______________ Fax _______________
Escrow Number: _______________

LENDER Name of officer _______________ □ **APPROVED**
Company _______________
Address _______________
Phone _______________ Fax _______________
Loan Number: _______________

TITLE COMPANY Name of Firm _______________ □ **COMPLETE**
Contact _______________
Phone _______________ Fax _______________

INSPECTION Service: _______________ Inspector: _______________

APPRAISAL Company _______________ Appraiser _______________

CLOSING DATE/LOCATION NOTIFICATION □ Buyers □ Sellers □ Agents □ Attorneys

□ "Just Sold" postcards
□ Housewarming Gift

"Thank You" Letters to: □ Buyers □ Agents □ _________
□ Sellers □ Lender

SUMMARY

There are three types of customer-buyers: focused buyers, browsers and window shoppers, each of which has a different degree of seriousness about buying a home. The assistant is often the first contact between a potential buyer and the agent. It's the assistant's responsibility to screen the buyers and to gather information about their preferences and financial situation through a buyer information sheet and prequalification process.

How a buyer comes to the agent can help determine his or her level of interest in buying. The assistant has a number of responsibilities toward buyers as customers, and more significant duties when the agent is a buyer's agent.

A purchase agreement is the document that makes a property transfer happen. The offer-and-acceptance cycle of negotiation is the process that leads to the purchase agreement. An assistant's first task after a buyer's offer is accepted is to help the agent handle the earnest money deposit in compliance with office policy and state law.

KEY TERMS

browsers
buyer information sheet
commingle
earnest money
focused buyers
prequalification
property value study (PVS)
purchase agreement
walk-ins
window shoppers

Review Questions

Questions 1 through 4 are based on the following facts:

Doris was out shopping one day, when she passed the office of Golden Threshold Realty. In the window, she saw a photo of a house in her neighborhood, so she went in to ask the agent about the asking price.

1. Based on *just the facts provided above,* Doris is a

   a. focused buyer. c. browser.
   b. window shopper. d. client

2. Doris currently rents an apartment, and has been saving to buy a home for several years. She knows she want to live somewhere in the city. Doris is a

   a. focused buyer. c. browser.
   b. window shopper. d. client.

3. Doris has sold her own house and is anxious to find a new one in the same neighborhood. *At the time she walks in the door*, Doris is a

   a. focused buyer. c. browser.
   b. window shopper. d. client

4. Golden Threshold Realty is a buyer's brokerage office. Doris signs an agency agreement with Alicia Agent. Doris is a

   a. client. c. window shopper.
   b. customer. d. buyer-customer.

5. One way to accurately determine whether a walk-in is a willing and able buyer is to ask them to complete a

   a. PVS
   b. buyer information sheet.
   c. purchase agreement.
   d. buyer showing sheet.

6. Which of the following does a buyer packet *not* contain?

   a. Agency disclosure information
   b. Marketing materials about the agent
   c. A comparative market analysis
   d. Information about the community

7. An assistant's responsibilities toward a buyer-customer include which of the following?

   a. Preparing a property value study
   b. Keeping the buyer's financial information strictly confidential
   c. Researching and reporting on the seller's motivations for moving.
   d. Scheduling showings of properties.

8. A "PVS" is a

   a. Prospective Verification Sheet.
   b. Property Valuation Sheet.
   c. Purchaser Validation Study.
   d. Property Value Study.

9. A seller who makes a counteroffer is

   a. accepting the buyer's original offer.
   b. rejecting the original offer with no further action.
   c. rejecting the buyer's offer and making his or her own new offer.
   d. accepting the buyer's original offer, but suggesting an improvement in its terms.

10. Broker *G* received an earnest money check from a buyer. *G* gave the check to his assistant, to deposit it in *G*'s personal checking account. The assistant should

    a. refuse to commingle the earnest money deposit with the agent's own funds.
    b. deposit the earnest money in her own account for safekeeping.
    c. deposit the check as instructed by *G*.
    d. put the check in a desk drawer.

12

Closing the Real Estate Transaction

In this chapter, we will discuss the final phase of a real estate transaction, and the assistant's role in coordinating lenders, appraisers and inspectors, and ensuring that the necessary documents are complete and present at the closing.

We will also discuss the assistant's role in the escrow process, and post-closing activities for which the assistant is responsible. By the end of the chapter you should have a clear idea of the closing and escrow procedures, and be able to identify the necessary parties and documents.

CLOSING IN GENERAL

The final stage of a real estate transaction is the **closing**: the point at which ownership of the property is transferred in exchange for payment of the purchase price. "Closing" is also known as *settlement*, *transfer*, or *passing papers* in various parts of the country.

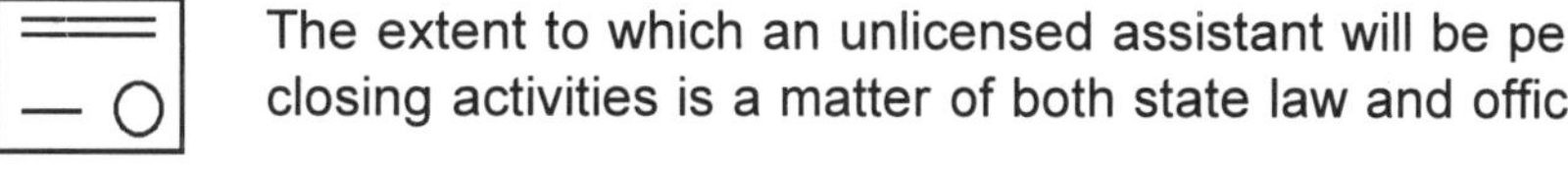

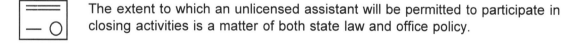

The extent to which an unlicensed assistant will be permitted to participate in closing activities is a matter of both state law and office policy.

Face-to-Face Closing and Closing in Escrow

There are two type of closings: in a **face-to-face closing**, the parties gather at a designated place and close the transaction in person. A face-to-face closing may be held in the offices of the title company, lending institution, one of the parties' attorneys, the broker, the county recorder or the escrow company. Persons who customarily attend a face-to-face closing include the buyer and seller, the real estate salespersons or brokers (and/or their assistants), the buyer's and seller's attorneys, and representatives of the lender and title insurance company. The parties sit around a conference table and pass around documents to sign until the transaction is complete.

The other type of closing is **closing in escrow**. In an escrow closing, a neutral third party (usually an attorney, title company, or the escrow department of a lending institution) is authorized by the parties to act as **escrow agent** (or *escrow holder*). Either the buyer or seller selects the escrow agent, depending on local practice or state law. Both the buyer and seller execute instructions to the escrow agent. The broker turns over the buyer's earnest money to the escrow agent, and the buyer and seller sign all the necessary documents and give them, along with the purchase price, to the escrow agent as well. The escrow agent's job is to sort out the documents, examine the title evidence, and conduct the transfer. If everything is in order, the escrow agent then gives the buyer title to the property, and turns the cash over to the seller.

The Real Estate Agent's Role

Depending on local practice, the real estate agent's role at a face-to-face closing may vary from simply collecting the commission to actually conducting the proceedings. However, because the real estate broker or salesperson is the contractual representative of one of the parties, he or she cannot be a neutral escrow agent. In any case, the broker is responsible for making sure that all the details are taken care of so the closing can proceed smoothly. This includes making arrangements for title evidence, surveys, appraisals, and inspections or repairs.

THE REAL ESTATE ASSISTANT'S ROLE

Obviously, the closing responsibilities of the real estate assistant will depend on the role customarily played by the agent. If the agent takes a very active role in preparing and conducting the closing, the assistant will be responsible for more details than if the agent's job is simply to show up and collect the commission check.

In either case, the assistant will be responsible for seeing to it that the closing proceeds smoothly and efficiently. This is mostly a matter of making sure that the right documents get to the right people, that inspections are scheduled and that everyone is aware of schedules and deadlines.

Closing in Escrow

In an escrow closing, the assistant is often responsible for coordinating the transaction with the closing or escrow agent: making sure the escrow agent is aware of time frames and special provisions, for example, and ensuring that documents and the earnest money deposit get to the escrow agent on time.

The necessary documents include:

- Purchase contract
- Listing agreement
- Earnest money statement, check and receipt

- Home protection contract
- Powers of attorney
- Existing loan information
- Escrow instructions

Figure 12.1 provides a detailed checklist for closing in escrow.

Lender Coordination

Most real estate transactions involve some sort of financing: most buyers do not have the full purchase price in cash, but have to borrow the money. Money borrowed to finance the purchase of real estate is called a **mortgage**: the lender provides the borrower with the necessary funds; in return, the borrower agrees to pay back the loan, with interest, over time, and offers the property as security for the loan. Most mortgages are paid back over fifteen or thirty years. The rate of interest may be either *fixed* or *adjustable*. In a fixed-rate mortgage, the interest rate is agreed upon when the borrower applies for the mortgage, and does not change during the life of the loan. In an adjustable-rate mortgage, the rate begins at a specific level, and then is raised or lowered periodically — such as annually or every six months — over the life of the loan.

There are a wide variety of financing methods and types of mortgages available. While both real estate agents and their assistants need to be familiar with them, it is important to be able to direct buyers to competent professional mortgage brokers and lending consultants who can give borrowers a better idea of the financing options available. An assistant should try to build relationships with good mortgage brokers and consultants, and keep their names and phone numbers of on file.

Immediately after the buyer's offer is accepted, the assistant should be able to provide him or her with the names and phone numbers of professional mortgage brokers and reliable lenders. A **mortgage broker** is a person who, for a fee, brings lenders and borrowers together. In effect, the mortgage broker helps the borrower fill out the application materials, and then brings the application to a lender for processing. The broker may "shop" the application among several lenders, looking for the lowest interest rates or most favorable terms.

The buyer should have been *prequalified* by the real estate agent (see Chapter 11). However, prequalification is not the same as being approved for a loan. Mortgage brokers may offer **pre-approval** for qualified buyers, however. This refers to the broker taking certain key financial information from the buyer (often over the phone), and then issuing a letter stating that the buyer will be able to be approved for the loan amount necessary for a specific purchase price. Real estate agents often like to have pre-approval letters with them when they present an offer to a seller, because it makes the buyers appear reliable.

When an agent represents the buyer, the assistant's responsibilities are considerably greater than when he or she works for a seller's agent. An assistant who works for a seller's agent will want to make sure that the buyer's agent is making the necessary loan arrangements quickly.

Figure 12.1 Countdown to Close of Escrow

Event	Goal Date	Actual Date
Contract acceptance by decision makers		
Property inspection by buyer		
Promissory note inspection and approval		
Service contract approval		
Escrow instructions prepared		
Escrow instructions signed		
Deposit submitted		
Deposit clears		
Professional property inspection		
Inspection results accepted		
Estoppel certificates approved		
Termite inspection		
Deposit increase to escrow		
Preliminary title report approval		
City approvals obtained		
Loan submitted to lender		
Appraisal performed		
Appraisal obtained		
Insurance obtained		
PMI approval		
Other contingencies cleared (specify)		
Formal loan approval		
Loan documents signed		
Funds submitted for down payment		
Close of escrow		
Buyer's occupancy		

An assistant should keep in regular contact with the lender in order to keep up with time frames and deadlines, and to head off problems before they get out of hand. The buyer should be encouraged to submit any information or materials the lender needs in a timely manner. When VA or FHA mortgages are involved, the assistant should allow extra time for the longer processing periods and more complex application procedures.

Insurance

Prior to closing, the buyer will need to acquire a homeowner's policy insuring the new house against losses and damage due to fire and other hazards. The insurance company will need sufficient time to view the property and process the application. Other forms of insurance may also be required by the lender, including flood or earthquake insurance.

Appraisal

Unless the lender is handling it, the assistant may be responsible for arranging the property appraisal. An **appraisal** is a formal estimate of the quality or value of a property, performed by a professional (and often state-licensed) appraiser based on standard methods of valuation. Its purpose is to determine whether or not the lender could sell the property for a value equal to the mortgage loan in case the borrower defaults (that is, fails to pay back the mortgage). In other words, the lender wants to know if the property is worth at least as much as the loan amount. Because so many transactions depend on the buyer obtaining a loan, the appraisal is an important part of the process.

The assistant will need to:

- ❖ coordinate with the appraiser to have access to the property — the appraiser must view both the interior and exterior of a home
- ❖ meet the appraiser at the property — either the assistant or the agent must be present during the appraisal to answer any questions or deal with any complications (such as locked doors or inaccessible areas)
- ❖ provide any assistance required by the appraiser
- ❖ supply the appraiser with recent comps, blueprints and plats

In the event that the appraisal comes out unsatisfactorily — for instance, valuing the property at less than the purchase price or loan amount — the assistant will need to help the agent arrange for a second appraisal, or reconsideration.

Inspections

It is important to adhere to the time periods specified in the purchase agreement for inspections. A **contingency** is a provision in the purchase agreement that requires a certain act to be performed or a particular event to occur before the contract is legally binding. Mortgage approval is a contingency, for instance. Property inspections are also common contingencies. It is in the best interests of the parties that the contingencies by satisfied, and all conditions lifted, as soon as possible. Inspections should be arranged almost immediately after a contract is signed (See Figure 12.2).

Home inspection. Most buyers will want to have a professional home inspector examine the property, both for hidden defects and simply to understand the nature of the property being purchased.

The assistant should schedule the inspection for a time convenient for both buyers and sellers — the buyers, who pay for the inspection, should be present, and the buyer's agent or assistant will need to be present during the inspection as well. The sellers should not be home.

Once the inspection is complete, the inspector will give the buyers a detailed report. If the sale is contingent on a satisfactory home inspection report, the attorneys and the parties will need to decide if the report raises questions or problems.

If the inspection uncovers significant defects, the buyer may demand that they be repaired. The assistant may need to arrange for written estimates of repair costs from a number of different providers, as well as for the actual work itself. The purchase agreement should specify whether the seller will pay directly for certain work, or if the cost will be deducted from the purchase price at closing.

Home inspection is a delicate matter: a sloppy inspection can miss material defects that will cause legal problems later, while a too-thorough inspection that emphasizes a property's negatives (particularly in the case of older homes) can scare off a buyer and ruin (or "crater") the sale. The assistant should check with his or her agent before arranging an inspection: does the agent have a preference regarding inspectors? Are there certain inspectors who should be avoided at all costs?

Termite inspections. Termite inspections and inspections for other pest infestations are usually valid for only 30 days from the inspection date, so the assistant should exercise care in scheduling them.

Environmental inspections. The contract (or state or local law) may require one or more environmental inspections. These include inspections for the presence of lead paint, radon gas and toxic waste or buried underground storage tanks (USTs). A toxic waste or UST inspection is particularly important in many commercial real estate transfers, or where a residential property is built on a site formerly used for industrial purposes (or certain potentially polluting commercial uses, such as gas stations and funeral homes). Most environmental inspections are conducted by private inspection companies.

Contractor inspection. Buyers may want to have certain parts of the property inspected by contractors to determine the extent of damage, the quality of workmanship or the cost of repair or replacement. In this case, the assistant may need to schedule visits by contractors and arrange for their access to the property. The agent or assistant should be present during contractor inspections.

Sewer, septic and wastewater inspection. Many states have laws regulating sewer, septic and wastewater systems. In such states, an inspector will need to certify the quality of the existing system, and may require it to be upgraded or connected to a municipal system.

Figure 12.2 Inspection Schedule — Checklist

TYPE OF INSPECTION	PROVIDER	DATE	REPAIR OR OTHER ACTION REQUIRED	DATE
Home Inspection				
Environmental:				
Lead Paint				
Radon Gas				
Underground Storage Tank				
Termite Inspection				
Contractor Inspection				
Sewer/Septic/ Wastewater				
Walk-Through				
OTHER INSPECTIONS:				

Disclosures

The doctrine of *caveat emptor* ("let the buyer beware") no longer applies to much of the typical real estate transaction. There are a variety of disclosures that must be made under state and federal law to ensure that all parties are treated fairly, have access to important information, and are generally playing on a level field. Some of the disclosure forms that it may be necessary for the assistant to have signed and available in the closing file include:

- *Seller's Property Disclosure Statement* — More and more states are requiring that sellers disclose known material defects in their properties before a buyer commits to a purchase. Lenders and title insurance companies may require proof that the disclosure was received by the buyer (see Chapter 1).

- *Agency Disclosures* — Many states also require that all parties to a transaction sign a form stating that the various agency relationships involved in the transaction have been explained to them (see Chapter 1).

- *Environmental Disclosure and Hazard Booklets* — State laws may require that special publications be distributed to buyers. In addition, the Department of Housing and Urban Development (HUD) requires distribution of a booklet about lead paint hazards in certain transactions.

- *Local Disclosures* — Municipalities may require disclosure of factual or safety information regarding certain structural features (such as swimming pools) or geological conditions (earthquakes, floods or land subsidence).

- ***Foreign Investment in Real Property Tax Act (FIRPTA)*** disclosure — The purpose of FIRPTA is to prevent foreign property owners from selling property in the United States and avoiding the income tax consequences of their profits. This federal law requires sellers to certify that they are U.S. citizens, or else pay an up-front 10 percent tax on the proceeds of the sale. Some exemptions apply to this complex tax law; an attorney should always be consulted.

- ***Real Estate Settlement Procedures Act (RESPA)*** disclosure — RESPA is a federal law that prohibits the payment or receipt of kickbacks and certain referral fees for activities involved in real estate finance. The law requires certain disclosures to consumers about any business relationships between real estate agents and mortgage lenders.

- Lender's disclosures — Mortgage lenders are required to provide consumers with a written ***good faith estimate*** of the total cost of the loan, including processing and administration fees. The federal **Truth-in-Lending Act** (also referred to as **Regulation Z**) requires lenders to disclose to borrowers the specific terms and conditions of the loan, including the amount financed, finance charges, the annual interest rate, the total amount that will be paid over the life of the loan, and any non-payment, late-payment or prepayment penalties.

Other Pre-Closing Activities

In addition to ensuring that disclosure forms are signed and filed, and that inspections are scheduled and follow-up action taken, the assistant may have a number of additional tasks prior to closing day. Figure 12.3 covers many of the details.

Title report. An assistant's other pre-closing responsibilities may include ordering the title report or abstract. When doing so, the assistant should be sure to request copies of all liens, encumbrances and deed restrictions that may be attached to the title. These are referred to collectively as **Schedule B items**. The assistant should be able to read and review the documents to see if there are any unexpected liens, or items that must be paid off prior to closing.

Buyer's walk-through. Immediately prior to closing, within no more than a day or two, the buyer should conduct a walk-through of the property. The **walk-through** is the buyer's final opportunity to inspect the property before he or she becomes its new owner. The buyer should use the walk-through as an opportunity to ensure that:

- the seller has moved out, or is preparing to move out in accordance with the terms of the sales contract
- all repairs or replacements that were included in the sales contract or that were required following an inspection have been adequately performed
- no damage has been done to the property by the current owner
- all items of personal property (such as light fixtures, window treatments and appliances) that are to convey to the buyer are still on the property and in good repair.

If the property has been damaged, or if property has been removed or altered without authorization, the buyer has the right to withhold part of the purchase price to cover repair or replacement.

The assistant should schedule the walk-through as close to the closing as possible. The agents for both the buyer and the seller, and/or their assistants, should attend the walk-through. The seller may also be present to answer questions. The seller's presence will depend largely on whether or not the transaction is proceeding in a friendly manner.

Schedule closing. Whether the closing is in escrow or face-to-face, it will take place at a certain time on a certain day. One of the parties, or their attorneys, will select a closing time. The assistant should be sure to contact all parties to remind them of the closing date, and make any appointments necessary to reserve office space or facilities.

Provide documents. All during the pre-closing period, the assistant should have been keeping track of which documents were still being prepared by the title company, lender or attorneys. As documents were completed, the assistant should have assembled them in a closing file for the property, making copies for the buyer or seller, depending on which party is being represented by the agent. The assistant should distribute all necessary documents to the

Figure 12.3 Forms and Information Required for Closing — Checklist

- ☐ AGENCY DISCLOSURE
- ☐ APPLIANCE/SYSTEM MANUALS
- ☐ GARAGE DOOR OPENER
- ☐ BILL OF SALE
- ☐ CERTIFICATE OF TITLE
- ☐ EARNEST MONEY DEPOSIT
- ☐ *FIRPTA* REQUIREMENTS
- ☐ GUARANTEES OR WARRANTIES
- ☐ HOMEOWNER'S INSURANCE
- ☐ KEYS
- ☐ MORTGAGE LENDER
- ☐ MORTGAGE NOTE
- ☐ MORTGAGE HISTORY
- ☐ PLAT OF SURVEY
- ☐ PROPERTY TAX BILLS
- ☐ PURCHASE PRICE STATEMENT
- ☐ QUITCLAIM DEED
- ☐ RELEASE OF JUDGMENT / LIEN
- ☐ *RESPA* REQUIREMENTS
- ☐ SALES COMMISSION
- ☐ SATISFACTION OF MORTGAGE
- ☐ SELLER DISCLOSURE
- ☐ STATEMENT OF POSSESSION
- ☐ ATTORNEY'S FEE STATEMENT
- ☐ TAX HISTORY
- ☐ TAX MATERIALS
- ☐ TITLE COMPANY FEE
- ☐ TITLE EXPENSE REPORT
- ☐ TITLE INSURANCE
- ☐ TRUTH-IN-LENDING DISCLOSURE
- ☐ UTILITY INFORMATION
- ☐ VENDOR'S AFFIDAVIT
- ☐ WALK-THROUGH
- ☐ WARRANTY DEED

OTHER:

closing agent or title company, as well as providing copies to the parties to give them time to read and question them before, rather than during, the closing.

Coordinate transfers. The assistant may assist the parties in efficiently transferring utility accounts (such as water, electricity, gas and telephone services). In addition, the buyer (or seller) may need some reminding about setting up (or stopping) mail and newspaper delivery, cable television service, and other details that are easily overlooked. The assistant may also facilitate key transfers, and the real estate office may provide a convenient location for dropping off spare keys, garage door openers and important manuals or phone numbers that got misplaced in the hectic final days of closing and moving.

The yard sign, lockbox and display materials should be removed from the house prior to closing.

Thank-yous and gifts. It is traditional for agents to maintain cordial professional relationships by sending thank-you notes to the other agent, the attorneys, the lenders and mortgage broker, the title company, and escrow agent. Anyone else who provided good service and expedited the transaction, such as a home inspector or appraiser, should also receive a thank-you letter. This responsibility frequently falls to the assistant. The letter should be specific (mention something that the recipient did or said that was particularly helpful or memorable) and brief. It should express appreciation without being sloppily sentimental. The example in Figure 12.4 follows a good pattern.

If the agent worked with the buyer, either as a customer or client, he or she may want to give the new owner a small housewarming gift. This should be obtained prior to closing, so the agent can make the presentation as soon as the last papers are signed. The assistant may be expected to purchase an appropriate gift, either in a local store or through a catalog specializing in business gifts.

POST-CLOSING

Once the transaction has closed, the assistant's responsibilities shift to clean-up and debriefing. **Clean-up** does not refer to tidying the office (although the assistant's desk could probably use some work: closings generate a lot of paper). Rather, it involves

- organizing the closing papers and other documents into the appropriate files
- making sure the files are in order and properly placed in the filing system
- adding necessary index lines to the file index
- closing out the computer files on the transaction, and entering the date of the closing so a happy-anniversary letter may be sent automatically to the buyers next year
- removing the listing from the MLS
- generating "Just Sold" postcards for a mailing to the agent's farm

Debriefing simply means the assistant should sit down with the agent and discuss the transaction, from start to finish. You should consider the following questions:

- ❖ What did we do right?
- ❖ What did we do wrong?
- ❖ What did the assistant (and the agent) learn from this transaction?
- ❖ How can you apply what you learned to transactions going on right now?
- ❖ How can you apply what you learned to future transactions?
- ❖ How could you have improved the transaction?

The answers to these questions will help the assistant grow in his or her profession. The assistant should write a memo detailing the answers and profiling the transaction, and the memo should be place in the transaction files, as well as in the assistant's personal file.

Figure 12.4 Thank-you Letter

LAKESIDE REALTY SERVICES, INC.

34 East Crescent Road — New Springs, West Carolina 01234

from *Ben Broker,* *ABR, CRS*

June 10, 1996

Ms. Alicia Agent
Golden Threshold Realty, Inc.
1515 Marigold Centre Drive
Centerton, West Carolina 01012

Dear Alicia:

As usual, I enjoyed working with you on the sale of 1984 Upton Place. It's always a rewarding experience to see a true professional at work. I was particularly impressed by the way you handled the home inspection issues: the Glendenning's were lucky to have you around!

The next time you're out here in the boonies, give me a call and we'll have lunch.

See you soon!

Sincerely,

Ben

Ben Broker

BB:pa

SUMMARY

The final stage of a real estate transaction is the closing: the point at which ownership of the property is transferred in exchange for payment of the purchase price. Closings may be face-to-face or in escrow. Regardless of which method is used, the assistant's role is to facilitate the closing by scheduling the pre-closing activities, such as inspections; coordinating lenders, insurance companies, and appraisers; and ensuring that the proper forms, documents and disclosures are distributed, signed and ready for closing day. After the closing is complete, the assistant should make sure the files are complete and organized, and should sit down with the agent to analyze what was done right and what was done wrong in the transaction.

KEY TERMS

appraisal
clean-up
closing in escrow
closing
contingency
contractor inspection
debriefing
environmental inspection
escrow agent
face-to-face closing
Foreign Investment in Real Property Tax Act (FIRPTA)
good faith estimate
home inspection
mortgage
mortgage broker
pre-approval
Real Estate Settlement Procedures Act (RESPA)
Regulation Z
Schedule B items
sewer, septic and wastewater inspection
termite inspection
Truth-in-Lending Act
walk-through

Review Questions

1. The final stage of any real estate transaction is the

   a. purchase and sale agreement.
   b. home inspection.
   c. closing.
   d. clean-up.

2. When a sale closes in escrow,

   a. the buyer and seller meet in the title company's office.
   b. a third party completes the mortgage application.
   c. a third party sorts out the documents, examines the title, and conducts the transfer.
   d. the assistant has no responsibilities.

3. A buyer applied for a mortgage through a mortgage broker. Under the terms of the loan, the buyer would pay interest at a rate of 7.5 percent for 30 years. This type of mortgage is called a/an

   a. fixed-rate mortgage.
   b. adjustable mortgage.
   c. regular mortgage.
   d. broker's mortgage.

4. When a prospective buyer provides a mortgage broker with certain financial information prior to making an offer, he or she want to be

   a. prequalified.
   b. pre-approved.
   c. prelisted.
   d. prebrokered.

5. Agent *O* represents the seller, and Agent *B* represents the buyer. In the pre-closing period, whose assistant has more to do?

   a. Agent *O*'s assistant
   b. Agent *B*'s assistant
   c. Both assistants will be equally busy.
   d. An unlicensed assistant may not legally do anything.

6. An appraisal is a/an

   a. informal valuation method used to determine a range of listing prices.
   b. inspection prior to closing, designed to uncover defects and learn about the exact condition of the property.
   c. formal estimate of the value of a property, performed by a professional to determine if the property is sufficient security for a loan.
   d. lender's formal statement of the total cost of a loan, including processing and administration fees, which must be given to a borrower under FIRPTA.

7. Broker *N* told Assistant *H*, "The contract on the *J* house is full of contingencies." What did Broker *N* mean?

   a. Assistant *H* will have to rewrite the contract to correct numerous errors.
   b. The *J* house is full of flaws, and will require much repair.
   c. The contract will not be final until certain provisions are satisfied.
   d. The contract contains deductions from the purchase price to cover specific repairs and replacements.

8. Toxic waste, USTs and radon gas are conditions that would be discovered in what kind of inspection?

   a. Contractor
   b. Environmental
   c. Septic
   d. Home

9. FIRPTA, RESPA and Regulation Z all require

   a. appraisals.
   b. inspections.
   c. disclosures.
   d. insurance.

10. A walk-through should occur immediately

    a. prior to clean-up.
    b. prior to closing.
    c. after an offer.
    d. after closing.

For Further Study…

The following materials provide in-depth discussion of many of the issues examined in this book. For more information call Real Estate Education Company® at 1-800-621-9621 *or visit our website at* http://www.real-estate-ed.com.

PROFESSIONAL SKILLS DEVELOPMENT

The Real Estate Agent's Business Planning Guide, *by Carla Cross* — Solid business planning techniques can help agents and assistants direct their activities, analyze their business and measure performance. A proven system developed by a nationally known speaker, author and award-winning real estate educator. Includes over 50 worksheets and checklists. Softcover, 256 pages. Order #190711-01

Real Estate Ethics, *3rd Edition, by William H. Pivar and Donald L. Harlan* — Both lively and thought-provoking, this book requires readers to evaluate problems, relationships and hypothetical situations from a liability point of view. Softcover, 192 pages. Order #196601-03.

Essentials of Real Estate Finance, *8th Edition, by David Sirota* — This text prepares readers to apply finance concepts to finance issues that they encounter every day in the real estate business. Numerous examples and exercises reinforce the student's ability to understand and use the information presented. Softcover, 352 pages. Order #155710-08.

Houses: The Illustrated Guide to Construction, Design & Systems, *2nd Edition, by Henry S. Harrison* — This clearly illustrated analysis of the real estate industry's primary "product" has sold over 300,000 copies. Includes styles, improvements, plans and problems. Softcover, 494 pages. Order #191315-02

Multiply Your Success With Real Estate Assistants, *by Monica Reynolds* — A hands-on guide for hiring, training and supervising real estate assistants. Softcover, 247 pages. Order #560888-01.

REFERENCE

Bienes Raíces: An English-Spanish Real Estate Dictionary — Adapted from the best-selling *Modern Real Estate Practice*, this dictionary is easy to use and understand, with more than 800 terms and translations. Softcover, 208 pages. Order #156501-01.

The Language of Real Estate, *4th Edition, by John W. Reilly* — The definitive reference guide to real estate terminology. Over 2,800 terms are clearly defined and cross-referenced, allowing users to grasp even complicated concepts easily. Softcover, 528 pages. Order #196101-04. *Also available on audiotape*

Realty Bluebook, *31st Edition, by Robert de Heer* — An essential reference tool for everyday practice, this book delivers on-the-spot answers to thousands of real estate questions. Its compact size makes it the real estate professional's constant companion. Softcover, 672 pages. Order #196510-31.

REAL ESTATE PRINCIPLES AND PRACTICE

Modern Real Estate Practice, *14th Edition, by Galaty, Allaway and Kyle* — A classic guide to real estate principles and practice and the nation's #1 principles text. Softcover, 433 pages. Order #151001-14.

Mastering Real Estate Principles, *by Gerald R. Cortesi* — A unique workbook-style learning system helps you master real estate exam material quickly and efficiently. Softcover, 532 pages. Order #151008-01.

Questions and Answers to Help You Pass the Real Estate Exam, *4th Edition, by Reilly and Vitousek* — The best-selling exam guide. Over 1,700 questions. Softcover, 316 pages. Order #197004-04.

Answer Key

Check your answers to the Review Questions found at the end of each chapter. If you did not answer a question correctly, restudy the material until you understand the correct answer.

CHAPTER 1

1. b
2. d
3. c
4. b
5. c
6. a
7. d
8. a
9. b
10. a

CHAPTER 2

1. d
2. c
3. c
4. a
5. b
6. a
7. c
8. b

CHAPTER 3

1. c
2. d
3. b
4. b
5. b
6. b
7. b
8. c
9. d
10. c

CHAPTER 4

1. c
2. d
3. b
4. c
5. a
6. d
7. c
8. b
9. a
10. a

CHAPTER 5

1. a
2. c
3. b
4. d
5. c
6. a
7. d
8. a
9. b
10. b

CHAPTER 6

1. c
2. d
3. c
4. b
5. c
6. a
7. a
8. a
9. d
10. b

CHAPTER 7

1. a
2. c
3. b
4. a
5. c
6. b
7. a

CHAPTER 8

1. c
2. a
3. b
4. d
5. b
6. c
7. b
8. c/d

CHAPTER 9

1. b
2. a
3. c
4. c
5. d
6. a
7. c
8. b
9. b
10. c

CHAPTER 10

1. c
2. d
3. b
4. a
5. d
6. b
7. d
8. c
9. d
10. a

CHAPTER 11

1. b
2. c
3. a
4. a
5. b
6. c
7. d
8. d
9. c
10. a

CHAPTER 12

1. c
2. c
3. a
4. b
5. b
6. c
7. c
8. b
9. c
10. b

Glossary

A

activity log An efficiency and organizing tool that permits an assistant to plan long-term projects over time.

administration In-office work that supports *sales* and *marketing* activities, including processing paperwork and bills, scheduling, correspondence, and filing activities.

administrative assistant An individual who assists in performing general office functions.

agency A legal relationship established between a *principal* and an *agent*, in which the agent is authorized to represent the principal in certain transactions. Agency relationships may be either *express* or *implied*.

agenda A list, outline or schedule of points to be covered in a meeting.

agent In an *agency* relationship, the agent is the person to whom the *principal* delegates a responsibility or authority. The agent owes the principal certain *fiduciary duties*.

agents' open house An open house held for agents from the listing agent's office or for other agents, to *preview* the property.

alphabetical organization A system of arranging files on the basis of the order of the letters of the alphabet.

appraisal A formal estimate of the quality or value of a property, performed by a professional (and often state-licensed) appraiser based on standard methods of valuation.

ARA (Accredited Residential Assistant) The designation offered to real estate assistants who have demonstrated appropriate professionalism and completed prescribed training by the National Organization of Real Estate Assistants (NORA).

B

bi-fold To fold into two parts, such as a *newsletter* or *brochure* format.

bit The smallest possible measurement of a computer's memory. A bit is the on or off designation to which all information usable by a computer must be reduced.

blockbusting The action of inducing homeowners to sell their properties by suggesting that the entry of persons of a particular race or national origin into the neighborhood will adversely change the neighborhood's character and value.

brochure A printed booklet, pamphlet or single-page letter that provides simple, basic information about an agent or office in an attractive and readable way.

browser A service used to navigate more efficiently through a computer network such as the *Internet*.

browsers Serious buyers who know generally what they want, but who have not yet decided on a specific property or area.

buyer's broker A real estate broker who represents the interest of the buyer in a real estate transaction.

buyer packet A file or folder of materials that is distributed to potential buyers of property. The packet may contain information about the community, lenders, mortgage rates and particular properties.

buying assistant A professional real estate assistant who specializes in facilitating real estate transactions strictly on behalf of buyers.

byte The basic unit of measurement for a computer's memory capacity, composed of eight bits, or on/off designations.

C

CE see continuing education

cellular phone A cordless, portable telephone that uses cells, or broadcast areas, instead of wires.

change form A general form used to record any alterations to a listing agreement.

checklist An organizing tool consisting of the steps in any process, arranged in order.

clean-up One of the last phases in an assistant's *closing* responsibilities: organizing files, closing out the listing and clearing out the transaction.

client A real estate agent's *principal*, whether the buyer or the seller. A client is owed the *fiduciary duties* of *agency*. All other parties in a transaction are the agent's *customers*.

client for life The principle that a real estate agent's goal should be to offer a client continuing services for all future transactions.

clipping file A file containing articles, publications and other materials relevant to the real estate profession.

closing The transaction in which ownership of a property is actually transferred.

closing coordinator A professional real estate assistant who specializes in organizing and facilitating closings.

closing in escrow A type of *closing* in which a neutral third party is authorized to collect the documents, review the transaction, and deliver title and the proceeds to the buyer and seller.

CMA *See* competitive market analysis

cold call A telemarketing call made randomly to an individual who does not expect to be called, to convey general information or to test market interest.

command keys Special keys on a computer's *keyboard* that provide shortcuts for having the computer perform special functions, such as running find-and-replace or spell check operations in a word processing program.

commingle The act of mixing together a buyer's *earnest money* deposit with the agent's own personal funds.

commission Usually a percentage of the selling price of a property, paid to the broker as *compensation* for services rendered in the sale or purchase of the property. The amount of commission payable is agreed between the parties in advance.

compensation A form of payment for services rendered. Compensation may be in the form of money, merchandise or other services.

competitive analysis A factual, statistical determination of the nature and identity of an agent's competitors.

competitive market analysis A comparison of the prices of recently sold properties that are similar in location, style and amenities to the listing seller's property. A CMA is an important tool in helping a seller determine an asking price.

contingency A provision in a purchase agreement that requires an act to be performed (such as a *home inspection*) or an event to occur before the contract is legally binding.

continuing education Courses that real estate licensees are required to take at certain intervals prior to renewing their licenses. CE course topics include current developments in real estate law and practice as well as reviews, refreshers and specialized real estate topics.

cooperating broker A competing broker who produces a potential purchaser for a property.

CPM A professional designation offered by the National Association of REALTORS®, CPM stands for "Certified Property Manager."

cross-reference A notation in one file indicating where additional or related information may be found in other files.

customer In a real estate transaction, a party who is not the agent's *client* is a customer. For example, where the agent represents the buyer, the buyer is the client and the seller is the customer. Customers are owed duties of reasonable care; honesty and fair dealing; and disclosure of all material facts.

D

daily planner An efficiency and organizing tool that helps an assistant keep track of his or her day-to-day responsibilities.

database A collection of information stored in a computer's memory that can be recalled and re-assembled in a variety of ways.

debriefing The final stage in an assistant's post-*closing* responsibilities, debriefing is simply sitting down with the agent and discussing the positives and negatives of the transaction just completed.

direct mail The marketing strategy of preparing individualized printed materials and mailing them to specific people in a targeted market.

disk drive The part of a computer system in which the computer's memory is located, and where calculations are performed, programs run and information retained.

download The process of having information transmitted from another computer to a user's through the *Internet*.

DREI A professional designation offered by the Real Estate Educators Association (REEA), which indicates the holder is a "Distinguished Real Estate Instructor." The designation is offered to outstanding real estate educators who also pass a written examination.

dual agency An agency relationship in which the agent represents both parties in the same transaction. Dual agency is generally considered unethical unless it is disclosed to both parties and both parties agree. Dual agency is illegal in many states.

E

E&O *See* errors and omissions insurance

e-mail Short for "electronic mail," a system of communicating between or among computers in a network or on the *Internet*.

earnest money A deposit made by a buyer to demonstrate his or her good faith intention to carry out the terms of the offer.

employee A person who is employed by another, and who is paid a regular salary, works under some supervision, receives benefits, and uses his or her employer's facilities and equipment.

errors and omissions insurance Policies required in some states, that protect brokers against liability for their own or their employees' errors, mistakes and negligence in the listing and selling of real estate. Known as "E&O" insurance.

escrow agent The neutral third party authorized to conduct a *closing in escrow*.

ethics A system of moral principles, rules and standards of conduct.

exclusive right to sell A form of *listing agreement* in which one broker is appointed as the sole representative of the seller to market the seller's property for a certain period of time.

exclusive agency listing A form of *listing agreement* in which the seller authorizes one broker as his or her representative, while retaining the right to sell the property without any obligation to pay the broker a *commission*.

exclusive buyer agency agreement An agreement in which a *buyer's broker* is hired by a buyer to represent the buyer's interests.

express agency An *agency* relationship which is established by a clear written or oral agreement between the parties.

F

face-to-face closing A type of *closing* in which the parties gather at a designated place and close the transaction in person.

Fair Housing Act A general term including Title VIII of the Civil Rights Act of 1968, the 1974 Housing and Community Development Act and the Fair Housing Amendments Act of 1988, prohibiting discrimination on the basis of race, color, religion, sex, handicap, familial status and national origin.

fair housing law A local, state or federal law that bans discrimination in housing.

farm The business region served by a real estate agent or assistant, which is cultivated for future clients.

fax A telephone-based communication system in which one machine converts hard copy into electronic signals and then transmits the signals over telephone lines to another fax machine, which converts them into *hard copy*.

Federal Communications Commission The federal government agency that regulates and controls telemarketing activities. Also known as FCC.

fiduciary duty The obligations owed by an *agent* to a *principal* in an *agency* relationship. The traditional fiduciary duties are care, obedience, accounting, loyalty and disclosure.

field In a *mail-merge* software program, the variable item to be inserted in a form or *direct-mail* letter.

fieldwork Any real estate related activity performed outside the office.

financing flier A *flier* prepared for a specific property that discusses mortgage interest rates, qualifying incomes and other financing issues.

FIRPTA *See* Foreign Investment in Real Property Tax Act

flier A single-page newsletter or brochure.

flowchart A graphic, step-by-step illustration of a *telemarketing* conversation, generally used in developing a *script*.

focused buyer A buyer who has found a specific property to buy, or who knows specifically where he or she wants to live.

font The style of type or letters used in designing printed material. Also referred to as *typeface*.

Foreign Investment in Real Property Tax Act (FIRPTA) A federal law designed to prevent foreign property owners from selling property in the U.S. without paying tax on the income.

four-step business management system A method of personal, task and office efficiency comprised of organization, anticipation, participation and measurement.

fraud The intentional misrepresentation of a material fact to take advantage of or harm another person. It includes making false statements as well as concealing or failing to disclose important facts.

FSBO Acronym for *F*or *S*ale *B*y *O*wner, pronounced "fizz-boe."

G

general agent In an *agency* relationship, a general agent is authorized to represent the *principal* in a broad range of matters, with great freedom of action.

good faith estimate Federally-required written statement of the total cost of a loan, processing and administration fees.

gratuitous agency A form of *agency* relationship in which the *agent* performs on behalf of the *principal* with no expectation of a fee or other *compensation*.

GRI A professional designation offered by the *National Association of REALTORS®*, GRI stands for "Graduate, REALTORS® Institute." It means the holder has successfully completed an approved course in a variety of professional interest areas, such as law, appraisal, finance and office management.

H

hard copy In a computer system, the materials produced by a *printer*. Also the product of a fax machine.

hardware The physical machines that make up a *computer system*.

headset A telephone receiver equipped with headphones and a small microphone that permits a telemarketer greater freedom of movement during calls.

home inspection A professional examination of a property to determine the presence of major or minor defects and to establish the need for repairs or replacements.

I

implied agency An agency relationship that is not established by an oral or written agreement, but in which the parties behave as if an agency relationship exists.

independent contractor A person who performs services for another, but who is not an *employee*. An independent contractor works more independently than an employee, pays all his or her expenses and employment taxes, and receives no benefits.

index Alphabetical list of topics that directs a user to the topic's location in a system.

input device Equipment that permits data to be entered into the computer's memory.

Internet A worldwide network of computers linked over telephone lines.

inventory A system of organization in which supplies, products or merchandise is listed in order to ensure that a sufficient quantity is always on hand or to keep track of the quantity available.

K

KB *See* kilobyte

keyboard In a computer system, an *input device* consisting of a board containing typewriter-like keys, along with specialized *command keys* for entering information into a computer's memory.

kilobyte (KB) A measurement of a computer's memory capacity, equal to 1,024 *bytes*.

L

laptop computer A lightweight, portable computer, generally weighing less than six pounds.

latent defect A hidden defect that would not be discovered by an ordinary inspection of the property.

learning base A file of personal progress reports, meeting notes, daily plans and checklists that permits an assistant to both track his or her progress and use past experience to resolve questions.

legislature The elected assembly of state government that creates the state real estate law, and grants a *real estate commission* the power to enforce the laws.

listing agreement An employment contract between a broker and seller of property. The listing agreement provides that the broker will perform his or her professional services in return for the payment of a *commission*.

listing coordinator An assistant who specializes in handling an agent's listings.

listing broker The broker from whose office a listing agreement is initiated.

listing packet An envelope or file folder that contains all the forms and documents an agent will need to list a home.

listing presentation book A marketing tool used by the agent to support and emphasize his or her oral listing presentation.

lock box A device attached to the door of a home, containing the house key. Lock boxes may be opened either mechanically (with a key) or electronically (with a keycard). A "smart lock box" keeps an electronic record of which agents visited the home.

long-term goals Job-related goals generally made up of a number of related tasks and *short-term goals* that may take many months.

M

macro-organizing Organizing on a large scale, such as whole office systems.

mail-merge A word processing software function that allows information from multiple documents to be combined into a single, *personalized* document.

market-driven An industry, such as real estate, in which services are provided to the public on the basis of the public's demand and desire for particular types of services.

market niche The part of the general real estate market which an agent dominates or seeks to dominate.

market posture The way in which an individual presents himself or herself to consumers in the marketplace.

market value The estimate of the most probable price that a property would bring in a transaction between a willing seller and buyer under normal conditions in the open market.

marketing The process by which sales are achieved. Marketing includes advertising both properties and services.

marketing assistant or **marketing coordinator** A professional real estate assistant who specializes in marketing both real estate and an agent, broker or office, including the design, production and distribution of advertising materials, programs and products.

marketing flier A *flier* produced for an individual property that features its statistics and amenities.

mass mailing The practice of sending identical letters or brochures to multiple recipients in a target market.

material defect A flaw that, were its existence known, would be likely to influence the buyer's decision whether to buy property.

megabyte (MB) A measurement of a computer's memory capacity, abbreviated *MB*, equal to 1,024 *kilobytes* or 1,048,576 *bytes*.

merged file In a *mail-merge* process, the document that contains both the form letter (*primary file*) and variables (*secondary file*); a *personalized* letter suitable for *direct mail*.

micro-organizing Organizing on a small scale, such as personal work habits or individual files.

MLS *See* Multiple Listing Service

modem An input/output device that permits a computer to send and receive information over a telephone line.

monitor In a computer system, the television-like screen on which information is displayed. An *output device*.

mortgage Money borrowed to finance the purchase of real estate, in which the land is pledged as security for the loan.

mortgage broker A person who brings together lenders and borrowers for a fee.

mouse A small, palm-shaped *input device* attached to a computer that permits a user to manipulate the image of an arrow or cursor on the *monitor* screen.

multiple listing service A marketing organization whose broker/members make their own exclusive listings available to each other. MLS listings may be found on computer networks as well as in a catalog.

N

NAR *See* National Association of REALTORS®

NAREB *See* National Association of Real Estate Brokers

National Association of Real Estate Brokers A professional association of real estate professionals. The 5,000 members of NAREB are known as *Realtists*.

National Association of REALTORS® The largest of the professional organizations in the real estate industry. Its 800,000 members subscribe to a *Code of Ethics* designed to ensure the fair and honest treatment of the public and other professionals. Members of NAR are the only persons entitled to be called *REALTORS®*.

net listing A form of *listing agreement* in which an amount of money is specified as what the seller receives from the sale. The broker may offer the property at any greater price, and is entitled to keep any amount over the seller's entitlement.

newsletter A form of printed marketing material; a tool for providing information that readers will find interesting while at the same time creating market awareness of an agent's presence and services.

noncompetition clause A contractual agreement in which one party agrees to practice real estate in a different area.

NORA The National Association of Real Estate Assistants, an organization founded to professionalize, educate and designate assistants. *See* ARA.

notebook printer A small, portable electronic printing device.

O

open-ended question In *telemarketing*, a question that cannot be answered with a simple yes-or-no response.

open listing A form of *listing agreement* in which the seller retains the right to employ several brokers simultaneously, and to market the property by him or herself as well. The seller is obligated to pay a *commission* only to the broker who produces the buyer.

operating system The software that is the computer's basic intelligence: operating systems tell a computer how to run itself and other programs most efficiently.

optical scanner In a computer system, an input device that permits printed material, including text, illustrations and photographs, to be transferred into a computer's memory.

option listing A form of listing agreement in which the broker receives the right to purchase the property.

output device In a computer system, a device such as a monitor or printer that permits the information in a computer's memory to be displayed or communicated by the computer in human-readable form.

P

pager A small electronic device carried by an agent that keeps him or her in contact with the office or others by transmitting an audible signal and/or a message.

palmtop computer A calculator-sized computer with limited memory capacity, offset by portability and convenience.

paperflow The way in which any document moves from one person to another in an office.

personalized A generic form letter that is made to appear personal by the insertion of a specific individual name or personal reference.

phone-flow The way in which a telephone call or message is routed through an office to its recipient.

power of attorney A signed document that authorizes one person (called the *attorney-in-fact*) to act as an agent for another.

pre-approval A service offered by *mortgage brokers* in which the broker takes certain key financial information from a prospective buyer prior to an offer being made on real estate. If the prospective buyer meet certain lending criteria, the broker will write a pre-approval letter stating that the buyer qualifies for a specific loan, subject to certain conditions.

prelicense class A course of instruction in real estate principles and practice, which individuals must pass prior to sitting for their state's real estate license examination. The length and number of prelicense classes required is a matter of state law.

pre-listing packet A package or folder of information designed to market an agent's services to potential sellers.

pre-listing phase The period of time between a potential seller's first contact with an agent and the completion of the agent's listing presentation.

prepping The process of preparing potential sellers for an agent's listing presentation by making a good first impression and gathering important information.

prequalification The practice of determining a potential buyer's financial ability to purchase a property.

preview An agent viewing a property without a prospective buyer.

primary file In a *mail-merge* function, a form letter with blanks left for insertions from the list of variables (*secondary file*).

principal In an *agency* relationship, the principal is the person who hires and/or delegates a responsibility to the *agent*. The principal owes the agent the duties of *compensation* and cooperation.

printer An *output device* that converts a computer's electronic language into a *hard copy* form readable by humans.

professional goals An assistant's vision of his or her career plan.

property disclosure report A disclosure, usually required by state law, of a home's condition, intended to inform potential buyers of flaws and necessary repairs.

property manager A broker employed by an owner to market, lease or manage the day-to-day operations of the owner's property.

property value study An analysis similar to a CMA which determines the market value of a property from a buyer's perspective, based on comparable properties and probable expenses.

provider-driven An industry in which the provider of goods or services controls the market for those goods or services.

puffing Exaggerated or superlative comments or opinions that do not constitute *fraud*.

purchase agreement documents The forms required for a binding, legal agreement to purchase property.

PVS *See* property value study

R

real estate commission An agency of state government established by the *legislature* to write and enforce rules and regulations governing the real estate profession.

real estate salesperson A licensed professional who, for some sort of compensation, is employed or associated with a broker to perform certain activities with regard to a real estate transaction.

real estate broker A licensed professional who, for a fee or commission, acts as an intermediary for another person in the sale or purchase of real property.

Realtist A member of the National Association of Real Estate Brokers.

REALTOR® A member of the *National Association of REALTORS®*.

Regulation Z *See* Truth-in-Lending Act

S

sales The activity of listing and selling property, including showing properties to prospective buyers.

sales activity log A record of sales- and marketing-related activities relating to a particular property.

sales support The assistant's role in facilitating various aspects of a sale.

script The written text of a telemarketing conversation, including alternative statements permitting the telemarketer to respond to a prospect's questions or objections in a controlled, predetermined way.

search parameters The method used to locate and retrieve information from a computer's *database* by specifying particular characteristics sought.

segmenting Determining the various identifiable groups that make up a market.

self-promotion An agent's activities in *marketing* his or her services to the public.

shared documents Any paper in a file that has more than one party's signature.

short-term goals Goals an assistant sets for individual jobs on a day-to-day basis.

showing An agent's act in bringing a buyer through a property being offered for sale.

showing information form A form filled out by a seller and agent that establishes the basic policies and procedures for how the property will be shown to prospective buyers.

software Computer programs. The set of electronic commands that make computer hardware work.

special agent In an *agency* relationship, a special agent is authorized to represent the *principal* in only one specific act or transaction, under detailed instructions.

spreadsheet Computer *software* that produces financial chart, records and analyses, and that performs calculations, stores numbers, and can recall particular numbers for later use.

state real estate commission An agency of state government established by the *legislature* to write and enforce rules and regulations governing the real estate profession.

steering The illegal practice of showing home seekers properties only in particular areas, either to maintain or to change the character of a neighborhood.

stigmatized property A property in which a violent or scandalous event has occurred that might have a negative effect the property's value.

stylus In a computer system, a pen-like input device that permits drawings or handwritten materials to be input.

T

talking sign A yard sign placed in front of a home for sale that contains a small radio transmitter. Information about the home is broadcast in a small area over a special radio frequency.

targeting The use of advertising and marketing techniques tailored to appeal to certain specific, discreet segments of a market.

telemarketing The use of the telephone as an active marketing tool to present an agent's services directly to the public.

telemarketing assistant A professional real estate assistant who specializes in conducting telemarketing activities on behalf of a broker, agent or office.

transactional brokers Real estate brokers who provide buyers and sellers with the paperwork and objective professional guidance necessary to transfer ownership of real property without establishing an *agency* relationship.

tri-fold To fold into three sections, such as in *brochure* design.

Truth-in-Lending Act A federal law that requires lenders to disclose to borrowers the specific terms and conditions of a loan. Also referred to as *Regulation Z.*

typeface The style of print or *font* used.

V

vision statement A concise, comprehensive statement of a real estate agent's character and goals, used to determine a marketing strategy.

visual interest In graphic design, the way an element catches a reader or viewer's attention.

voice mail An electronic telephone answering system, as well as a message sorting, directing, storage and retrieval system.

W

walk-ins Prospective buyers who come to a real estate office in person.

walk-through The buyer's final opportunity to inspect property before closing

warm call A *telemarketing* call made with a specific purpose in mind, and which is relevant to a recipient's known interest in being contacted.

word processor Computer *software* that is used to create documents, letters and other written communications.

web sites On the *Internet*, computers that are linked to the information network.

window shoppers People who enjoy looking at houses but who have no intention of buying.

Index